CORE SKILLS

Math

ISBN 0-7398-5723-1

2002 Edition, Harcourt Achieve Inc.
Copyright © by Harcourt, Inc.

9 10 11 12 0982 11 10 09

Rigby • Saxon • Steck-Vaughn

www.HarcourtAchieve.com
1.800.531.5015

Core Skills: Math
Grade 1
Table of Contents

Core Skills: Math, Grade 1, Table of Contents (cont.)

Core Skills: Math, Grade 1, Table of Contents (cont.)

Sorting by Color and Size

Cut and paste.
Put in the object that belongs.

1.
2.
3.
4.

Visual Thinking

5. Where does the  belong? Ring the group.

Patterns

Ring to continue the pattern.

1.

2.

3.

4.

Reasoning

5. Which patterns are alike?
   Ring them.

A B A B A B	A B B A B B
A B B A B B	A A A A A A

2

Same, More, Fewer

1. Draw a group that has the same number.

△ △ △ △ △   △ △ △ △ △

---

2. Draw a group that has more.

□ □ □

---

3. Draw a group that has 1 more.

○ ○ ○ ○

---

4. Draw a group that has fewer.

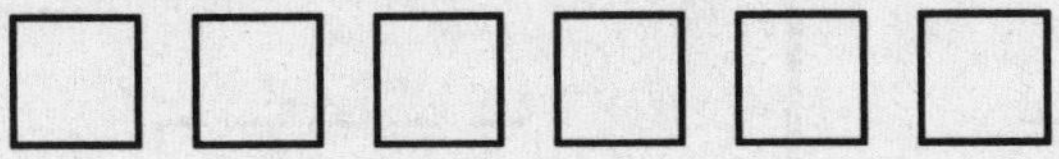

□ □ □ □ □ □

Number Sense

5. Which group has more?
   Ring the group.

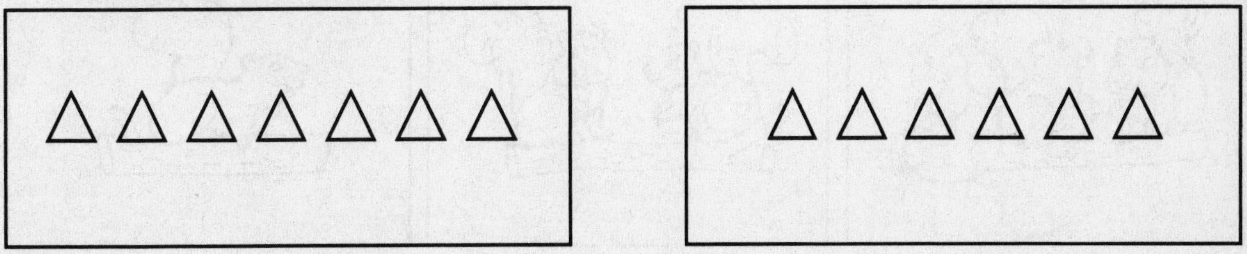

△ △ △ △ △ △ △   △ △ △ △ △ △

Two, One, Three

Ring each pair.

Put a counter on each bird.
Write how many.

1.

_2_

2.

_____

3.

_____

Number Sense

4. Which shows 1 more than a pair? Ring the group.

4

Four and Five

Write how many.

1.

5

2.

3.

Number Sense

4. Ring the group that has more than 3.

Draw an X on the groups that have the same number.

Counting Pennies

Write how much.

1. 3¢

2. _____ ¢

3. _____ ¢

4. _____ ¢

5. _____ ¢

6. _____ ¢

Number Sense

7. Look at each purse. Ring the purse that has more pennies. Draw an X on the purse that has fewer pennies.

Zero

Write 0.

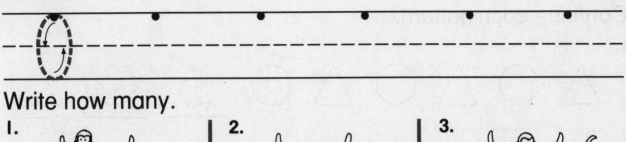

Write how many.

1.

3

2.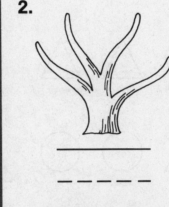

_____

3.

_____

4.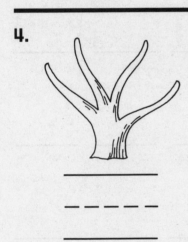

_____

5.

_____

6.

_____

Number Sense

7. Ring the group that has more than 4.
Draw an X on the groups that have the same number.

Problem-Solving Strategy

Draw a Picture

Continue each pattern.

I. △ ◯ △ ◯ △ ◯   △ ◯ △
___ ___ ___

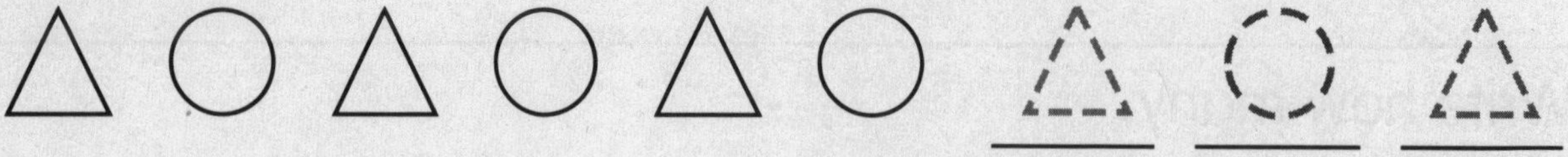

2. ◯ △ △ ◯ △ △
___ ___ ___

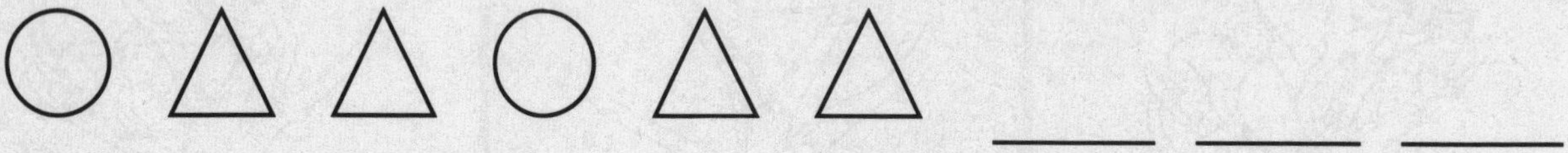

3. △ ◯ ◯ △ ◯ ◯
___ ___ ___

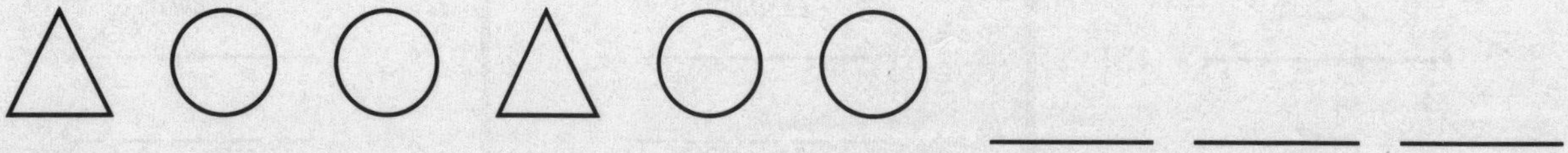

4. △ ◯ △ ◯ △ ◯
___ ___ ___

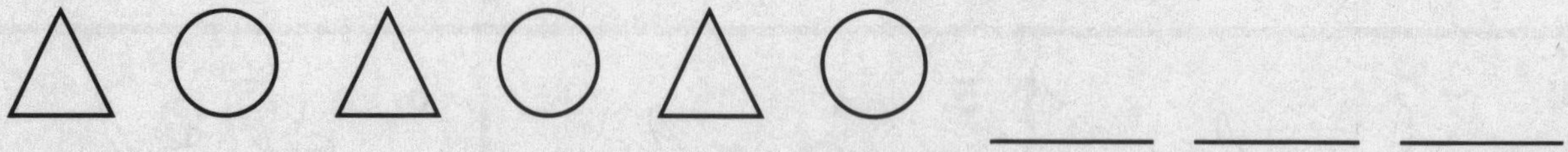

5. ◯ △ ◯ △ ◯ △
___ ___ ___

6. △ △ ◯ △ △ ◯
___ ___ ___

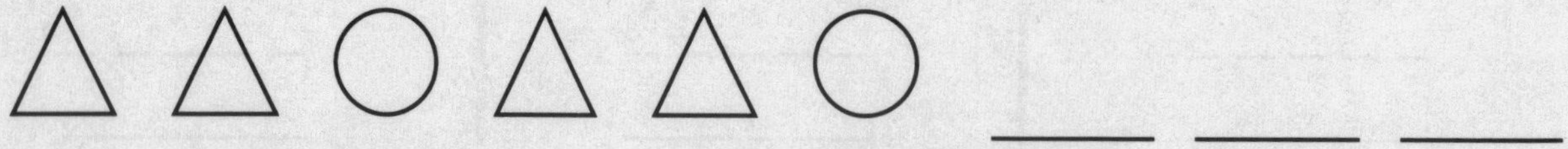

7. ◯ ◯ △ △ ◯ ◯
___ ___ ___

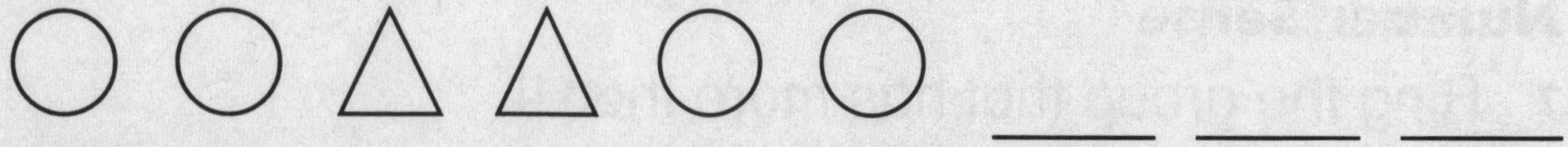

Reasoning

8. Do rows 3 and 6 show
the same pattern?
Ring **Yes** or **No**.

Yes   No

Six and Seven

Write how many. Ring the number word.

1.

_____6_____

five   (six)

2.

_____

four   five

3.

_____

zero   one

4.

_____

five   six

5.

_____

six   seven

6.

_____

two   three

Visual Thinking

7. Ring the groups that have more than 5.
Draw an X on the groups that have fewer than 5.

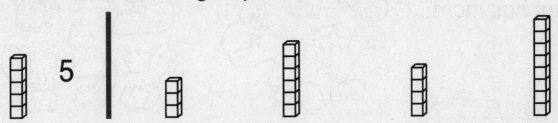

5

Eight and Nine

Which groups have 8? Ring them [red].

1.

Which groups have 9? Ring them [blue].

2.

Number Sense

3. Ring the group that has more.

Ten

Ring how many. Then write the number.

1.

   six

   (nine)

   ten

   9

2. five

   six

   seven

3. ten

   zero

   two

4. eight

   three

   one

Reasoning

5. Which group of dolphins has 2 fewer than 9?
   Ring the group.

Order Through 10

Write the number that comes next.

1. 3, 4, 5

2. 4, 5, _____

3. 8, 9, _____

4. 5, 6, _____

5. 0, 1, _____

6. 2, 3, _____

Count backward. Write the missing numbers.

7.

10, 9, ___, ___, ___, 5, 4, ___, 2, ___, 0

8.

10, ___, ___, 7, 6, ___, ___, ___, ___, 1

Number Sense

9. Ring the group that comes next.

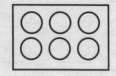 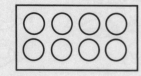 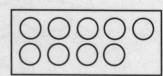 

Comparing Numbers

Write how many.
Then ring the number that is greater.

1.

6   5

2.

_____   _____

- - - - -   - - - - -

Write how many.
Then ring the number that is less.

3.

_____   _____

- - - - -   - - - - -

_____

4.

_____   _____

- - - - -   - - - - -

Story Corner

Complete the sentences. Use these words.

    six   **ten**   _____

                                      - - - - - -

5. Ten is greater than _____ .

                                      _____

                                      - - - - - -

6. Six is less than _____ .

Problem-Solving Strategy
Make a Pictograph

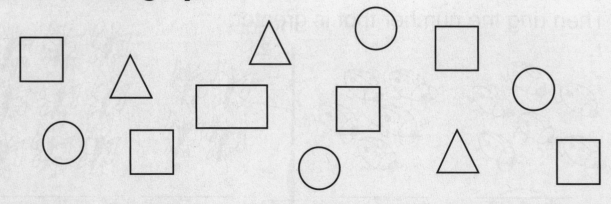

1. Count each shape.
   Draw shapes to complete the graph.

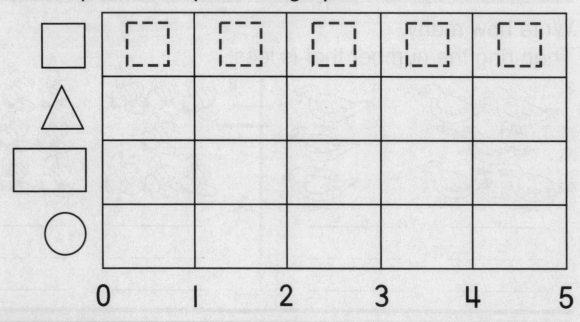

Reasoning

Look at the graph.

2. Ring the one with more.

3. Ring the one with fewer.

Understanding Addition

Tell a story to a friend. Write how many.

How many?	How many join?	How many in all?

1.

4   1   5

2.

_____   _____

3.

  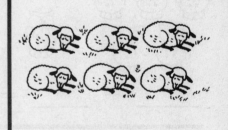

_____   _____   _____

Problem Solving

Make up a story. Write how many in all.

4.

_____

5.

_____

15

Addition Sentences

Write the addition sentences.

1.

$$\underline{}2 + \underline{}1 = \underline{}3$$

2.

$$\underline{\qquad} + \underline{\qquad} = \underline{\qquad}$$

3.

$$\underline{\qquad} + \underline{\qquad} = \underline{\qquad}$$

4.

$$\underline{\qquad} + \underline{\qquad} = \underline{\qquad}$$

5.

$$\underline{\qquad} + \underline{\qquad} = \underline{\qquad}$$

6.

$$\underline{\qquad} + \underline{\qquad} = \underline{\qquad}$$

Story Corner

7. Tell a story to a friend. Write an addition sentence.

$$\underline{\qquad} + \underline{\qquad} = \underline{\qquad}$$

Order in Addition

Use counters.
Draw X to show how many.
Write the sum.

1.

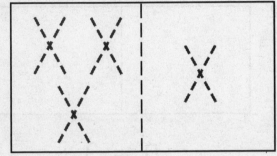

$3 + 1 = \underline{4}$

$1 + 3 = \underline{4}$

2.

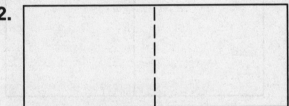

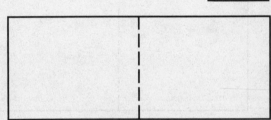

$2 + 4 = \underline{}$

$4 + 2 = \underline{}$

3.

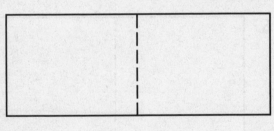

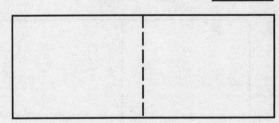

$4 + 1 = \underline{}$

$1 + 4 = \underline{}$

Reasoning

4. Ring the pair that shows the same number.

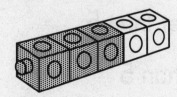 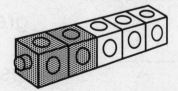 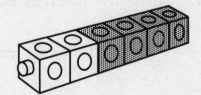

Adding 0

Use counters.
Draw dots to show how many.
Write the sum.

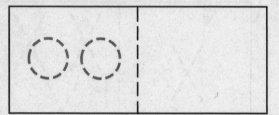

1. 2 + 0 = __2__

2. 0 + 3 = ___

3. 0 + 5 = ___

4. 1 + 0 = ___

5. 6 + 0 = ___

6. 0 + 4 = ___

Number Sense

7. Ring the better estimate.

4 + 0 = __?__

greater than 5

less than 5

18

Problem-Solving Strategy

Draw a Picture

Make up a story.
Complete the picture. Solve.

1.

$$2 + 1 = \underline{3}$$

2.

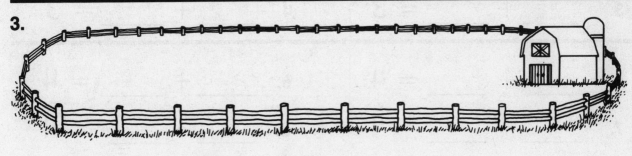

$$3 + 2 = \underline{}$$

3.

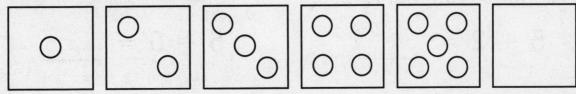

$$5 + 1 = \underline{}$$

Reasoning

4. Continue the pattern.

○	○ ○	○ ○ ○	○ ○ ○ ○	○ ○ ○ ○ ○	

19

Addition Combinations

Use counters. Find ways to make the sums.
Then write the addition sentences.

1. _____ + _____ = 3   2. _____ + _____ = 3

3. _____ + _____ = 3   4. _____ + _____ = 3

5. _____ + _____ = 4   6. _____ + _____ = 4

7. _____ + _____ = 4   8. _____ + _____ = 4

9. _____ + _____ = 4

Number Sense

10. Ring the sum that is less.

5 + 2 = _____   5 + 0 = _____

More Addition Combinations

Put in 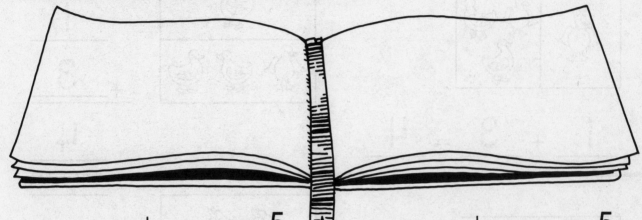.
Find ways to make the sums.

1. _____ + _____ = 5   2. _____ + _____ = 5

3. _____ + _____ = 5   4. _____ + _____ = 5

5. _____ + _____ = 5   6. _____ + _____ = 5

7. _____ + _____ = 6   8. _____ + _____ = 6

9. _____ + _____ = 6   10. _____ + _____ = 6

11. _____ + _____ = 6   12. _____ + _____ = 6

13. _____ + _____ = 6

Reasoning

14. Do both groups have the same number?
    Ring **Yes** or **No**.   Yes   No

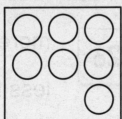   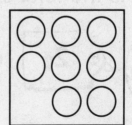

Vertical Addition

Complete.

1.

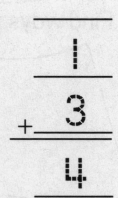

___1___ + ___3___ = ___4___

$$\begin{array}{r} 1 \\ +\ 3 \\ \hline 4 \end{array}$$

2.

_____ + _____ = _____

$$\begin{array}{r} \underline{} \\ +\ \underline{} \\ \hline \end{array}$$

3.

_____ + _____ = _____

$$\begin{array}{r} \underline{} \\ +\ \underline{} \\ \hline \end{array}$$

Number Sense

4. What is the total cost? Ring the better estimate.

 and

more than 5¢

less than 5¢

22

Problem-Solving Strategy

Act It Out

Read the story. Act it out.
Write the number sentence.

1. 3 girls walk.
   2 girls run.
   How many girls are there?

   $\underline{3} + \underline{2} = \underline{5}$

2. 4 girls smile.
   1 girl frowns.
   How many girls are there?

   _____ + _____ = _____

3. 5 girls play.
   0 girls work.
   How many girls are there?

   _____ + _____ = _____

4. 2 boys jump.
   2 boys hop.
   How many boys are there?

   _____ + _____ = _____

Visual Thinking

5. Ring the ones that have the same sum.

Understanding Subtraction

Tell a story to a friend. Write how many.

How many?	How many go away?	How many are left?

1.

3   1   2

2.

_____   _____   _____

3.

_____   _____   _____

Story Corner

4. Look at the picture.
   Write the missing numbers.

   I see —— boys.

   I see —— boy run away.

   I see —— boys left.

Subtraction Sentences

Write each subtraction sentence.

1.

4 — 2 = 2

2.

___ — ___ = ___

3.

___ — ___ = ___

4.

___ — ___ = ___

5.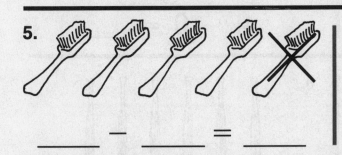

___ — ___ = ___

6.

___ — ___ = ___

Number Sense

Write each number.

7. How many faces? _____

How many 🙂 ? _____

How many 🙁 ? _____

8. How many faces? _____

How many 🙂 ? _____

How many 🙁 ? _____

25

Zero Property

Write how many are left.

1.

$$2 - 0 = \underline{\ 2\ }$$

2.

$$3 - 3 = \underline{\ \ \ \ }$$

3.

$$6 - 6 = \underline{\ \ \ \ }$$

4.

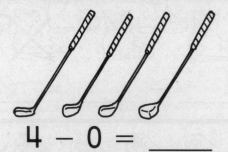

$$4 - 0 = \underline{\ \ \ \ }$$

5.

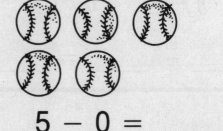

$$5 - 0 = \underline{\ \ \ \ }$$

6.

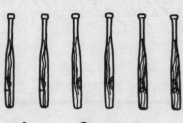

$$6 - 0 = \underline{\ \ \ \ }$$

7.

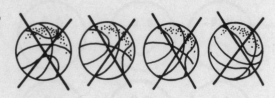

$$4 - 4 = \underline{\ \ \ \ }$$

8.

$$2 - 2 = \underline{\ \ \ \ }$$

Reasoning

9. You pick 3  .
You eat all but 1.
How many do you eat? _____ apples

More Subtraction Sentences

Cross out. Then write how many are left.

1.

    4 − 2 = __2__

2.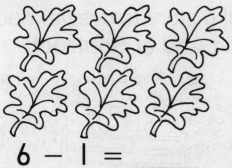

    6 − 1 = ____

3.

    5 − 2 = ____

4.

    4 − 1 = ____

5.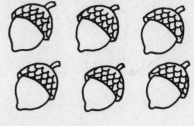

    6 − 2 = ____

6.

    5 − 0 = ____

Story Corner

7. Tell a story to a friend.
   Write the subtraction sentence.

____ − ____ = ____

Problem Solving

Choose the Operation

Tell a story to answer each question.
Ring **Add** or **Subtract**.

1.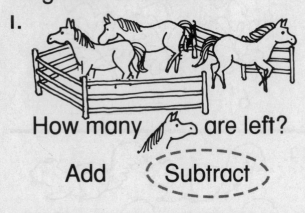

How many 🐴 are left?

Add ~~(Subtract)~~

2.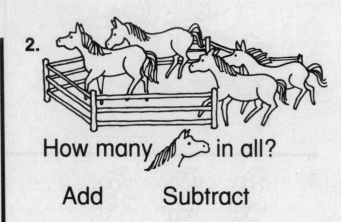

How many 🐴 in all?

Add   Subtract

Match each number sentence.

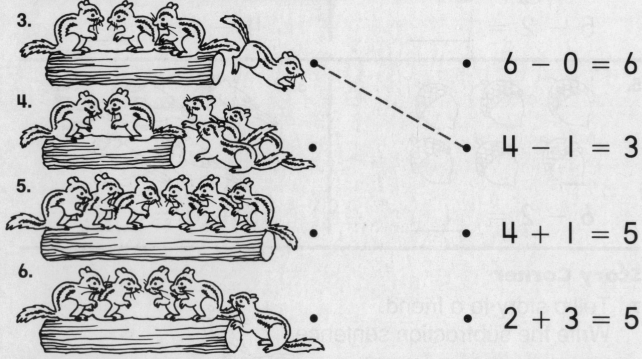

3. •   • $6 - 0 = 6$

4. •   • $4 - 1 = 3$

5. •   • $4 + 1 = 5$

6. •   • $2 + 3 = 5$

Reasoning

7. Write the missing sign.

$3 \bigcirc 3 = 6$ $3 \bigcirc 3 = 0$ $0 \bigcirc 3 = 3$

Subtraction Combinations

Put in 4 .

Find ways to subtract from 4.

1. $4 - \underline{2} = \underline{2}$ 2. $4 - \underline{} = \underline{}$

3. $4 - \underline{} = \underline{}$ 4. $4 - \underline{} = \underline{}$

5. $4 - \underline{} = \underline{}$

Subtract.

6. $3 - 1 = \underline{}$ $5 - 0 = \underline{}$ $4 - 4 = \underline{}$

7. $6 - 6 = \underline{}$ $2 - 1 = \underline{}$ $1 - 0 = \underline{}$

8. $4 - 3 = \underline{}$ $3 - 2 = \underline{}$ $6 - 4 = \underline{}$

9. $2 - 2 = \underline{}$ $5 - 2 = \underline{}$ $6 - 1 = \underline{}$

10. $3 - 0 = \underline{}$ $6 - 3 = \underline{}$ $1 - 1 = \underline{}$

Number Sense

Ring the better estimate.

11. $9 - 3 = \underline{}$ more than 9   less than 9

More Subtraction Combinations

Put in 5 .

[ ]

Find ways to subtract from 5.

1. $5 - \underline{5} = \underline{0}$ 2. $5 - \underline{} = \underline{}$

3. $5 - \underline{} = \underline{}$ 4. $5 - \underline{} = \underline{}$

5. $5 - \underline{} = \underline{}$ 6. $5 - \underline{} = \underline{}$

Look for a pattern. Subtract.

7. $6 - 3 = \underline{}$ $6 - 2 = \underline{}$ $6 - 1 = \underline{}$

8. $5 - 2 = \underline{}$ $5 - 1 = \underline{}$ $5 - 0 = \underline{}$

9. $5 - 1 = \underline{}$ $5 - 2 = \underline{}$ $5 - 3 = \underline{}$

10. $4 - 0 = \underline{}$ $4 - 1 = \underline{}$ $4 - 2 = \underline{}$

Number Sense

11. Which answer will be the least?
    Ring it. Then solve to check.

    $10 - 3 = \underline{}$ $10 - 2 = \underline{}$ $10 - 1 = \underline{}$

Vertical Subtraction

Subtract.

1.
$$\begin{array}{r} 4 \\ -2 \\ \hline 2 \end{array}$$

2.
$$\begin{array}{r} 5 \\ -1 \\ \hline \end{array}$$

3.
$$\begin{array}{r} 6 \\ -0 \\ \hline \end{array}$$

4.
$$\begin{array}{r} 4 \\ -3 \\ \hline \end{array}$$

5.
$$\begin{array}{r} 5¢ \\ -5¢ \\ \hline ¢ \end{array}$$

6.
$$\begin{array}{r} 6¢ \\ -1¢ \\ \hline ¢ \end{array}$$

7.
$$\begin{array}{r} 6¢ \\ -4¢ \\ \hline ¢ \end{array}$$

8.
$$\begin{array}{r} 5¢ \\ -4¢ \\ \hline ¢ \end{array}$$

Visual Thinking

9. Draw dots to continue the pattern.

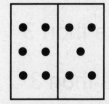 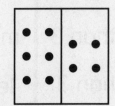 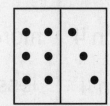 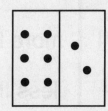 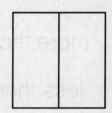

Addition and Subtraction

Add or subtract.

1.

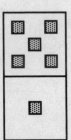

$$\begin{array}{r} 5 \\ + 1 \\ \hline 6 \end{array}$$

$$\begin{array}{r} 6 \\ - 1 \\ \hline \end{array}$$

$$\begin{array}{r} 6 \\ - 5 \\ \hline \end{array}$$

2.

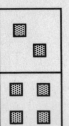

$$\begin{array}{r} 2 \\ + 4 \\ \hline \end{array}$$

$$\begin{array}{r} 6 \\ - 4 \\ \hline \end{array}$$

$$\begin{array}{r} 6 \\ - 2 \\ \hline \end{array}$$

3.

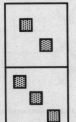

$$\begin{array}{r} 2 \\ + 3 \\ \hline \end{array}$$

$$\begin{array}{r} 5 \\ - 3 \\ \hline \end{array}$$

$$\begin{array}{r} 5 \\ - 2 \\ \hline \end{array}$$

Number Sense

4. Ring the better estimate.

$\begin{array}{r} 4 \\ +1 \\ \hline ? \end{array}$	$\begin{array}{r} 4 \\ -1 \\ \hline ? \end{array}$	$\begin{array}{r} 3 \\ +2 \\ \hline ? \end{array}$	$\begin{array}{r} 3 \\ -2 \\ \hline ? \end{array}$
more than 4	more than 4	more than 3	more than 3
less than 4	less than 4	less than 3	less than 3

Problem Solving

Choose the Question

Ring the correct question.

1. Rosa sees 3 🕊️ .
   Then all of them fly away.

   How many 🕊️ in all?

   (How many 🕊️ are left?)

2. Chad counts 5 🍄 .
   Then he sees 1 more.

   How many 🍄 in all?

   How many 🍄 are left?

3. Mrs. Davis finds 2 🌰 .
   Then she finds 2 more.

   How many 🌰 in all?

   How many 🌰 are left?

4. Mr. Davis sees 2 🐸 .
   Then 1 hops away.

   How many 🐸 in all?

   How many 🐸 are left?

5. Chad watches 4 🐿️ .
   Then 3 run away.

   How many 🐿️ in all?

   How many 🐿️ are left?

6. Rosa counts 3 🌿 .
   Then she counts 3 more.

   How many 🌿 in all?

   How many 🌿 are left?

Story Corner

7. Tell a story about the picture.
   Write the number sentence.

   ____ ◯ ____ ----- ____

Counting On

Count on to add. Write each sum.

1.

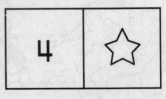

4 + 1 = __5__    4 + 2 = _____

2.

8 + 1 = _____   5 + 2 = _____

3.

5 + 1  = _____   2 + 2 = _____

4.

6 + 1 = _____   7 + 1 = _____   8 + 1 = _____

5.

8 + 2 = _____   7 + 2 = _____   6 + 2 = _____

Number Sense

6. Ring the one that has the greatest sum.

10 + 2   10 + 1   10 + 0

34

More Counting On

Count on to add. Write each sum.

1.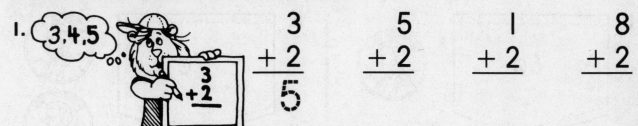

	3	5	1	8
	+ 2	+ 2	+ 2	+ 2
	5			

2.

2	5	8	1	9	7
+ 1	+ 1	+ 1	+ 1	+ 1	+ 1

3.

3	7	5	1	4	6
+ 3	+ 3	+ 3	+ 3	+ 3	+ 3

4.

7	5	9	8	6	6
+ 2	+ 3	+ 1	+ 2	+ 3	+ 2

5.

4	4	8	7	5	5
+ 3	+ 2	+ 1	+ 3	+ 2	+ 1

Number Sense

6. Ring the one that has the least sum.

9 + 2   9 + 1   9 + 3

Counting On 1, 2, and 3

Count on to add. Write each sum.

1.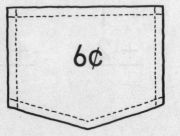

6¢ + 1¢ = __7__ ¢

2.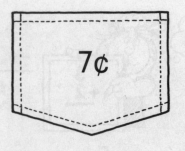

7¢ + 2¢ = ____ ¢

3.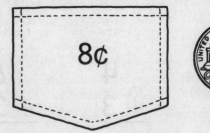

8¢ + 1¢ = ____ ¢

4.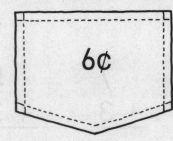

6¢ + 2¢ = ____ ¢

5.

4¢ + 3¢ = ____ ¢

6.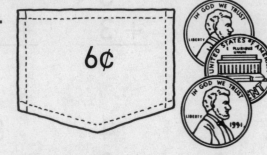

6¢ + 3¢ = ____ ¢

Reasoning

Solve.

7. Lee has 5¢.
   Kara has 3¢ more than Lee.
   Tom has 2¢ more than Kara.
   How much money does Tom have? ____¢

Problem Solving

Use a Picture

Write the addition fact to find the total amount.

1.

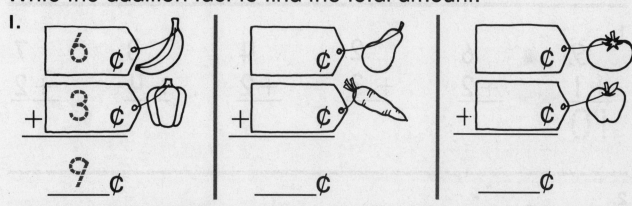

6 ¢	___ ¢	___ ¢
+ 3 ¢	+ ___ ¢	+ ___ ¢
9 ¢	___ ¢	___ ¢

2.

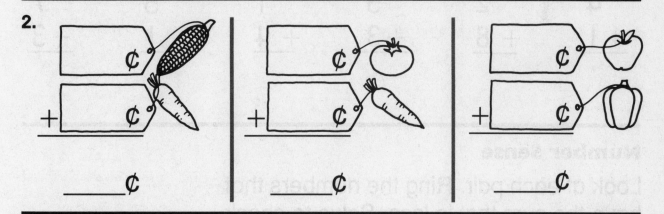

___ ¢	___ ¢	___ ¢
+ ___ ¢	+ ___ ¢	+ ___ ¢
___ ¢	___ ¢	___ ¢

Story Corner

3. Look at the picture.
   Make up a story problem.
   Tell it to a friend.
   Have a friend solve it.

Counting On

Mental Math

Ring the greater number. Then add.

(7) (8)
+ 1
8

2
+ (6) (7,8)
8

(6) (7,8,9)
+ 3
9

Look for the greater number. Count on from that number.

1.

(9)
+ 1
10

6
+ 2

2
+ 3

4
+ 2

3
+ 4

7
+ 2

2.

4
+ 1

2
+ 8

5
+ 3

1
+ 4

5
+ 1

7
+ 3

Number Sense

Look at each pair. Ring the numbers that
have the sum that is less. Solve to check.

3.
1   8
+ 8   + 2

4.
3   2
+ 5   + 5

5.
4   4
+ 3   + 2

38

Doubles

Complete each doubles fact.
Write each sum.

1. $4 + \underline{4} = \underline{8}$ | $1 + \underline{} = \underline{}$

2. $0 + \underline{} = \underline{}$ | $5 + \underline{} = \underline{}$

3.
$$\begin{array}{cccccc} 3 & 1 & 4 & 2 & 0 & 5 \\ +3 & +1 & +4 & +2 & +0 & +5 \\ \hline \end{array}$$

Write each sum. Ring each double.

4.
$$\begin{array}{cccccc} 2 & 7 & 3 & 0 & 6 & 5 \\ +6 & +1 & +3 & +0 & +3 & +5 \\ \hline \end{array}$$

5.
$$\begin{array}{cccccc} 4 & 3 & 5 & 2 & 2 & 1 \\ +4 & +7 & +3 & +2 & +5 & +1 \\ \hline \end{array}$$

Reasoning

Solve.

6. Chen has 3¢.
   Jon has double this amount.
   Mary has 1¢ more than Jon.
   How much money
   does Mary have? _____ ¢

Addition Table

Write the missing sums.

+	0	1	2	3	4	5	6	7	8
0	0	1	2		4	5		7	
1	1	2	3			6		8	9
2	2		4	5	6	7	8		10
3	3			7		9	10		
4	4	5	6		8	9			
5	5		7	8		10			
6	6	7		9					
7	7		9						
8	8		10						

Reasoning

Peter saw 3 red and 5 brown birds.
Jane saw 4 red and 4 brown birds.
Enrico saw 2 red and 7 brown birds.
Which children saw the same number of birds?

_____   _____

_____   _____

_____ and _____

40

Adding Three Numbers

Add. Start with the ringed numbers.

1. ③ + ③ + 4   3 + ③ + ④

   __6__ + __4__ = __10__   __3__ + __7__ = __10__

2. ② + ⑤ + 1   2 + ⑤ + ①

   ___ + ___ = ___   ___ + ___ = ___

Add.

3.
```
  1       4       3       6       1       1
  1       2       4       3       3       3
+ 8     + 2     + 1     + 1     + 5     + 3
```

4.
```
  4       1       2       3       1       6
  4       2       3       2       7       4
+ 1     + 7     + 4     + 5     + 1     + 0
```

Reasoning

5. Use doubles to add.
   Ring the numbers you would add first.

   1 + 5 + 4

   ___ + ___ = ___

Making Arrangements

Color 6 different 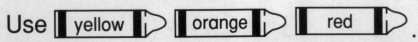.

Use ![yellow] ![orange] ![red].

Each part of the 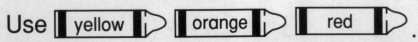 must be a different color.

1.

2.

3.

4.

5.

6.

Visual Thinking

7. Ring the two pictures that are the same.

Problem Solving

Too Much Information

Draw a line through the sentence you do not need. Then solve.

1. There are 4 cars on the road.
   ~~There are 2 trucks on the road.~~
   Then 3 more cars come.
   How many cars are there?

$$4 + 3 = 7$$

_____ 7 cars

2. Mr. Ladd sees 4 buses.
   Then he sees 4 more buses.
   He sees 1 train, too.
   How many buses does he see?

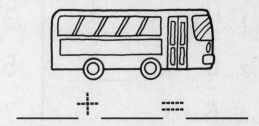

_____ + _____ = _____

_____ buses

3. Anna counts 5 trees.
   She counts 3 stop signs.
   Then she counts 6 more
   stop signs. How many stop
   signs does she see?

_____ + _____ = _____

_____ stop signs

Story Corner

4. Look at the picture.
   Make up a story problem.
   Tell it to a friend.
   Have a friend solve it.

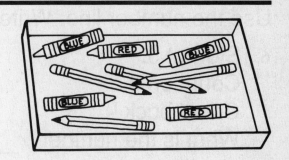

Counting Back

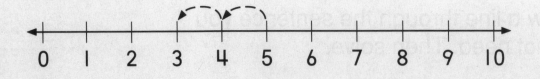

$$5 - 2 = \underline{3}$$

Use the number line. Count back to subtract.

  4,3   3,2   6,5,4

1. $4 - 1 = \underline{3}$ $3 - 1 = \underline{}$ $6 - 2 = \underline{}$

2. $6 - 1 = \underline{}$ $5 - 2 = \underline{}$ $8 - 1 = \underline{}$

3. $5 - 1 = \underline{}$ $7 - 2 = \underline{}$ $4 - 2 = \underline{}$

4. $9 - 2 = \underline{}$ $3 - 2 = \underline{}$ $10 - 1 = \underline{}$

5. $7 - 1 = \underline{}$ $9 - 1 = \underline{}$ $10 - 2 = \underline{}$

Number Sense

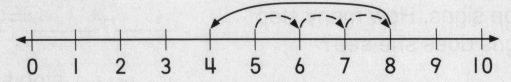

Use the number line. Write the number.

6. Start at 5.
   Count on 3.
   Count back 4.
   What is the number? ___

7. Start at 6.
   Count on 4.
   Count back 4.
   What is the number? ___

More Counting Back

$$\begin{array}{r} 9 \\ -1 \\ \hline 8 \end{array}$$ 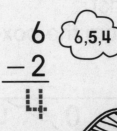 9, 8

$$\begin{array}{r} 7 \\ -2 \\ \hline 5 \end{array}$$ 7, 6, 5

$$\begin{array}{r} 6 \\ -2 \\ \hline 4 \end{array}$$ 6, 5, 4

Count back to subtract.

1.
$$\begin{array}{r} 8 \\ -1 \\ \hline \end{array}$$
$$\begin{array}{r} 10 \\ -1 \\ \hline \end{array}$$
$$\begin{array}{r} 4 \\ -1 \\ \hline \end{array}$$
$$\begin{array}{r} 5 \\ -1 \\ \hline \end{array}$$
$$\begin{array}{r} 3 \\ -1 \\ \hline \end{array}$$
$$\begin{array}{r} 6 \\ -1 \\ \hline \end{array}$$

2.
$$\begin{array}{r} 3 \\ -2 \\ \hline \end{array}$$
$$\begin{array}{r} 10 \\ -2 \\ \hline \end{array}$$
$$\begin{array}{r} 5 \\ -2 \\ \hline \end{array}$$
$$\begin{array}{r} 4 \\ -2 \\ \hline \end{array}$$
$$\begin{array}{r} 9 \\ -2 \\ \hline \end{array}$$
$$\begin{array}{r} 8 \\ -2 \\ \hline \end{array}$$

3.
$$\begin{array}{r} 7 \\ -1 \\ \hline \end{array}$$
$$\begin{array}{r} 9 \\ -2 \\ \hline \end{array}$$
$$\begin{array}{r} 9 \\ -1 \\ \hline \end{array}$$
$$\begin{array}{r} 6 \\ -2 \\ \hline \end{array}$$
$$\begin{array}{r} 5 \\ -1 \\ \hline \end{array}$$
$$\begin{array}{r} 7 \\ -2 \\ \hline \end{array}$$

Reasoning
Solve.

4. Mario is 5 years old.
   Sam is 2 years younger than Mario.
   Fumi is 1 year younger than Sam.
   How old is Fumi?

_____ years old.

45

Counting Back 1, 2, and 3

Count back to subtract.
Use your answers from the box to color
the picture blue.

1.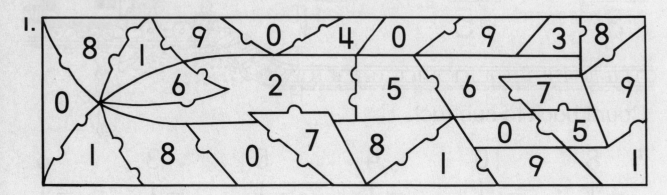

$4 - 2 =$ __2__ $8 - 1 =$ _____ $9 - 3 =$ _____

$8 - 3 =$ _____ $9 - 2 =$ _____ $7 - 1 =$ _____

$5 - 1 =$ _____ $6 - 3 =$ _____ $7 - 2 =$ _____

2.
$$\begin{array}{cc} 8 \\ -2 \\ \hline \end{array} \qquad \begin{array}{cc} 5 \\ -3 \\ \hline \end{array} \qquad \begin{array}{cc} 3 \\ -1 \\ \hline \end{array} \qquad \begin{array}{cc} 6 \\ -2 \\ \hline \end{array} \qquad \begin{array}{cc} 9 \\ -1 \\ \hline \end{array} \qquad \begin{array}{cc} 7 \\ -3 \\ \hline \end{array}$$

Number Sense

Look at each pair.
Ring the numbers that have the answer
that is less. Solve to check.

3.
$$\begin{array}{cc} 7 \\ -1 \\ \hline \end{array} \qquad \begin{array}{cc} 7 \\ -3 \\ \hline \end{array}$$

4.
$$\begin{array}{cc} 8 \\ -1 \\ \hline \end{array} \qquad \begin{array}{cc} 8 \\ -2 \\ \hline \end{array}$$

5.
$$\begin{array}{cc} 9 \\ -2 \\ \hline \end{array} \qquad \begin{array}{cc} 9 \\ -3 \\ \hline \end{array}$$

Problem-Solving Strategy

Make a Model

Use counters to solve.

1. There are 8  .

   Then 3 go away.

   How many are left?

   __5__

2. There are 5  .

   Then 2 go away.

   How many are left?

   _____

3. There are 7  .

   Then 2 go away.

   How many are left?

   _____

4. There are 8  .

   Then 2 go away.

   How many are left?

   _____

5. There are 6 .

   There are 3 .

   How many more

   than ?

   _____ more

6. There are 9 .

   There are 3 .

   How many more

   than ?

   _____ more

Story Corner

7. Make up two story problems about a .
   Tell them to a friend. Have your
   friend solve each one.

Subtracting Zero and Related Facts

Subtract. Write each difference.

1.
| 6
−1
5 | 6
−5
1 | 3
−0 | 3
−3 | 8
−3 | 8
−5 |

2.
| 9
−2 | 9
−7 | 4
−1 | 4
−3 | 10
−3 | 10
−7 |

3.
| 10
−2 | 10
−8 | 7
−2 | 7
−5 | 9
−3 | 9
−6 |

4.
| 7
−3 | 7
−4 | 5
−3 | 5
−2 | 10
−1 | 10
−9 |

Reasoning

Which boy is Terry? Ring him.
5. Jack has 3 balls.
Fred has 3 more balls
than Jack.
Terry has more balls
than Jack or Fred.

Addition and Subtraction

Write an addition fact. Cross out the black counters. Then write the subtraction fact.

1.

$$\begin{array}{r} 5 \\ +\ 1 \\ \hline 6 \end{array}$$

$$\begin{array}{r} 6 \\ -\ 1 \\ \hline 5 \end{array}$$

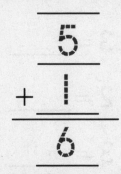

2.

$$\begin{array}{r} \\ +\quad \\ \hline \\ \hline \end{array}$$

$$\begin{array}{r} \\ -\quad \\ \hline \\ \hline \end{array}$$

3.

$$\begin{array}{r} \\ +\quad \\ \hline \\ \hline \end{array}$$

$$\begin{array}{r} \\ -\quad \\ \hline \\ \hline \end{array}$$

4.

$$\begin{array}{r} \\ +\quad \\ \hline \\ \hline \end{array}$$

$$\begin{array}{r} \\ -\quad \\ \hline \\ \hline \end{array}$$

Visual Thinking

5. Think about the picture.
   Ring **Add** or **Subtract**.

   Add   Subtract

49

Fact Families

Use cubes. Add or subtract.
Write the numbers in each fact family.

1. $5 + 1 = \underline{6}$ $3 + 1 = \underline{}$ $2 + 3 = \underline{}$

   $1 + 5 = \underline{6}$ $1 + 3 = \underline{}$ $3 + 2 = \underline{}$

   $6 - 1 = \underline{5}$ $4 - 1 = \underline{}$ $5 - 3 = \underline{}$

   $6 - 5 = \underline{1}$ $4 - 3 = \underline{}$ $5 - 2 = \underline{}$

   $\underline{5}, \underline{1}, \underline{6}$ $\underline{}, \underline{}, \underline{}$ $\underline{}, \underline{}, \underline{}$

Add or subtract.
Which sentence does not belong? Ring it.

2.

   $2 + 6 = \underline{}$

   $6 + 2 = \underline{}$

   $8 - 2 = \underline{}$

   $7 - 2 = \underline{}$

   $8 - 6 = \underline{}$

3.

   $5 + 3 = \underline{}$

   $3 + 5 = \underline{}$

   $4 + 3 = \underline{}$

   $8 - 5 = \underline{}$

   $8 - 3 = \underline{}$

Problem Solving

Write the numbers.

4. Our sum is 5. Our difference is 1. $\underline{}$ and $\underline{}$

Exploring Probability

What can happen when you toss 3 two-color counters? Ring each group that shows what can happen.

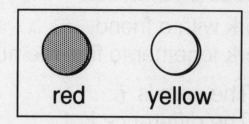
red   yellow

1.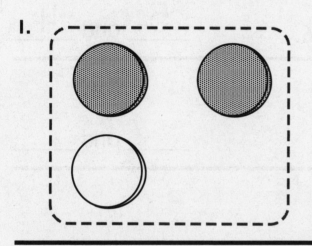

2.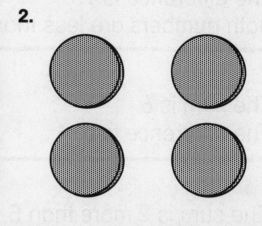

3.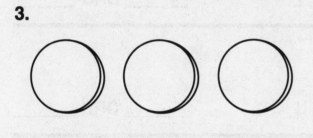

4.

5.

6.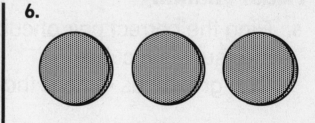

Problem Solving

7. Nick tossed 3 two-color counters.
   He tossed them 2 times.
   He got 4 red sides in all.
   How many yellow sides in all did he get? _____ yellow

Problem-Solving Strategy

Guess and Check

Work with a friend.
Work together to find the number pair.

1. The sum is 9.
   The difference is 1.
   Both numbers are less than 6.   __5__ and __4__

2. The sum is 6.
   The difference is 0.   _____ and _____

3. The sum is 2 more than 5.
   The difference is 1 less than 2.   _____ and _____

4. The sum is 1 more than 7.
   The difference is 2 less than 4.   _____ and _____

Visual Thinking

5. Ring the correct pair of cubes.
   The sum is 6 cubes.
   One group has 4 more than the other.

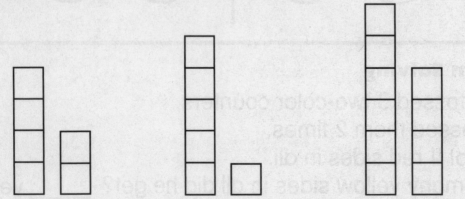

Solid Shapes

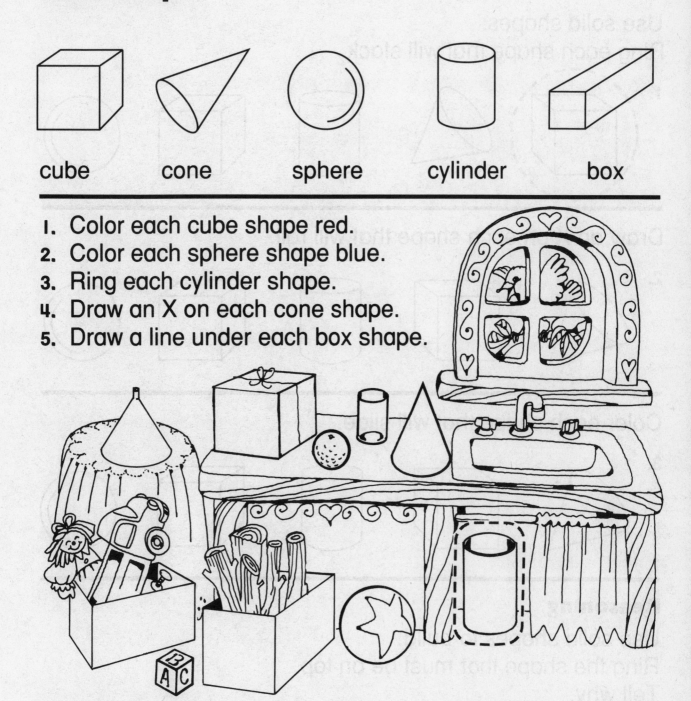

cube   cone   sphere   cylinder   box

1. Color each cube shape red.
2. Color each sphere shape blue.
3. Ring each cylinder shape.
4. Draw an X on each cone shape.
5. Draw a line under each box shape.

Story Corner

6. Read this riddle.
   Ring the name of the shape.
   I am a solid shape.
   All my sides are flat.

   cone   cube   sphere

More Solid Shapes

Use solid shapes.
Ring each shape that will stack.

1.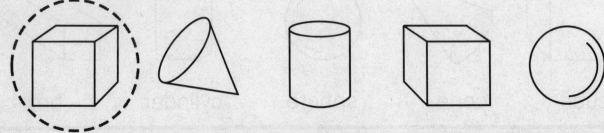

Draw an X on each shape that will roll.

2.

Color each shape that will slide.

3.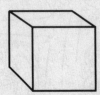

Reasoning

Use solid shapes to build.
Ring the shape that must be on top.
Tell why.

4.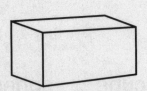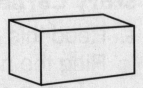

54

Solid and Plane Shapes

Match the plane shape to the solid.

1.

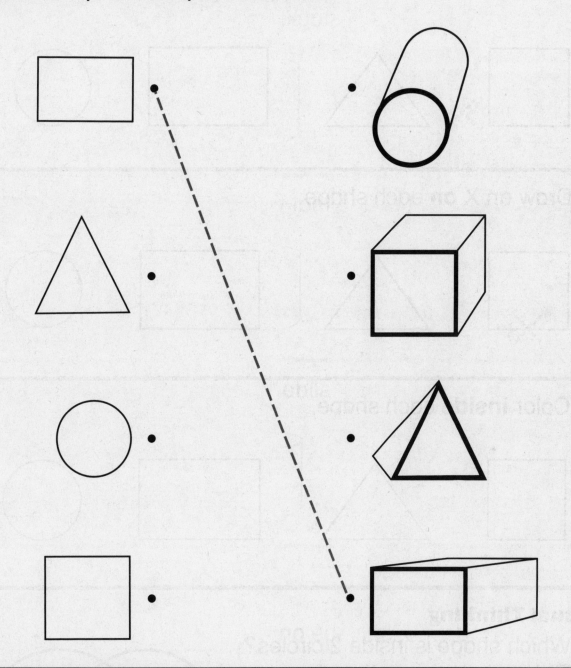

Visual Thinking

2. Count the △ .
   Write how many.

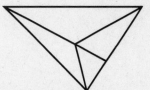

_____

Inside, Outside, On

1. Draw an X **outside** each shape.

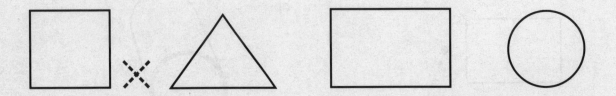

2. Draw an X **on** each shape.

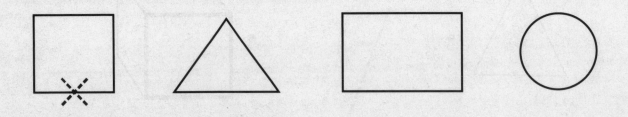

3. Color **inside** each shape.

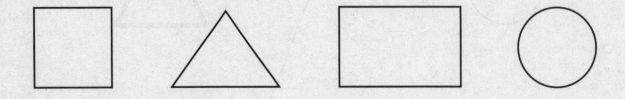

Visual Thinking

4. Which shape is inside 2 circles?
Ring the shape.

Open and Closed Figures

Color inside each closed figure.
Ring the figures that are open.

open   closed

1.

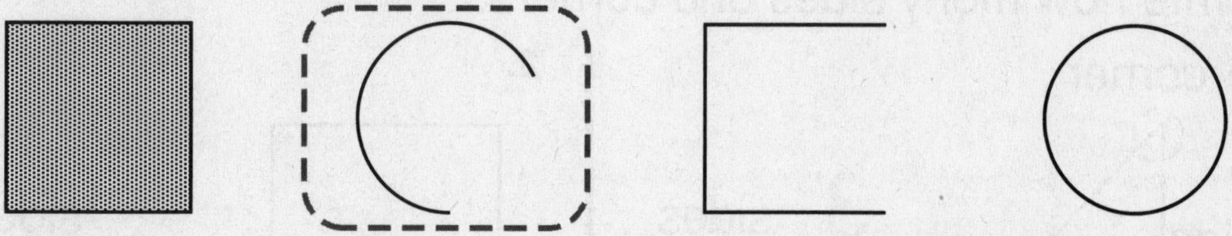

2.

Color inside each rectangle.

3.

Visual Thinking

4. Ring the letters that are open figures.

C D G N O S

Sides and Corners

Trace each side 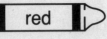 .

Draw a  ⬭ on each corner.

Write how many sides and corners.

1. corner

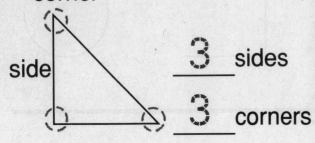

side

__3__ sides

__3__ corners

2.

_____ sides

_____ corners

3.

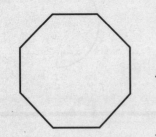

_____ sides

_____ corners

4.

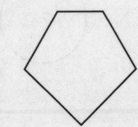

_____ sides

_____ corners

5.

_____ sides

_____ corners

6.

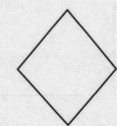

_____ sides

_____ corners

Reasoning

7. What kind of figure
has 2 sides and 1 corner?   open figure   closed figure
Ring the answer.

58

Problem-Solving Strategy

Make a Bar Graph

Count the shapes. Complete the graph.

1.

	0	1	2	3	4	5	6	7	8

Story Corner

2. Read this riddle. Draw the shape.
   I am an open figure. I have 4 sides.
   I am a letter between T and X. _____

Symmetry

Draw a line to make two parts that match.

1.

2.

3.

4.

5.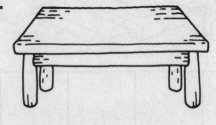

6.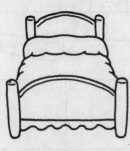

7.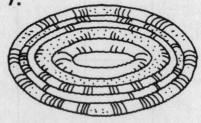

8.

Visual Thinking

9. Ring the two parts that do **not** match.

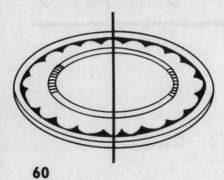  

Congruent Figures

Ring the ones that are the same shape and size. Use punch-out shapes if you need to.

1.

2.

3.

4.

Story Corner

5. Compare the figures to the first one.
   Ring the correct word.

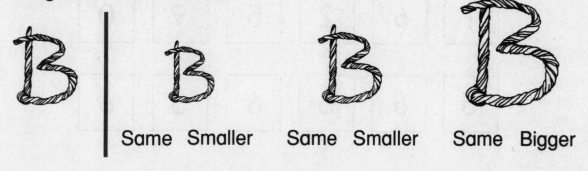

Same Smaller   Same Smaller   Same Bigger

Patterns

Match to continue each pattern.

1.

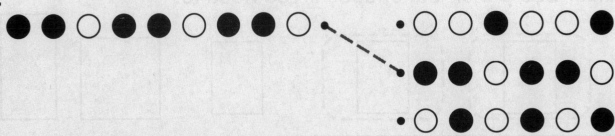

2.

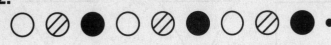

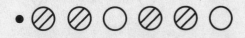

3.

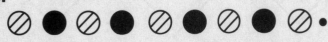

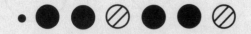

Number Sense

4. Draw a line under the row
that shows a number pattern.

| 1 | 6 | 2 | 5 | 9 | 0 |

| 5 | 6 | 5 | 6 | 5 | 6 |

62

More Patterns

Color the stars to continue the pattern.

Color R stars red.

Color B stars blue.

1.

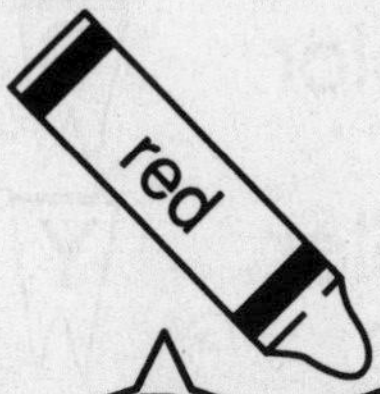

2.

3.

Number Sense

4. Write a number to continue the pattern.

4   1   2   4   1   2   4   1   2   4   ____

Problem-Solving Strategy

Find a Pattern

Read each pattern. Color the .

Color 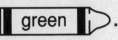 blue .

Color green .

Color 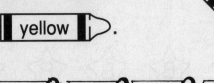 yellow .

1.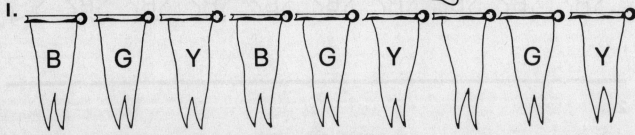

B G Y B G Y G Y

2.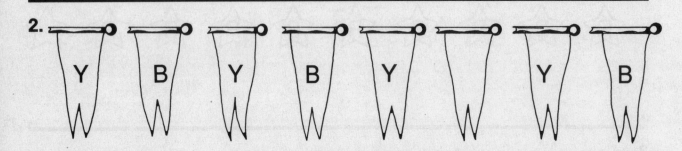

Y B Y B Y Y B

3.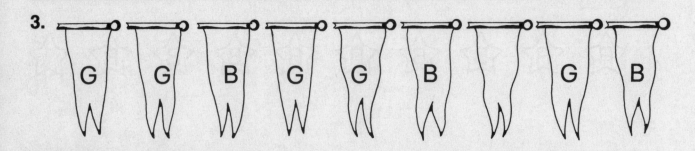

G G B G G B G B

Number Sense

4. Ring the missing number.

9   2   9   2   9   __?__ | 9   4   2

Groups of 10

Ring groups of 10.
Write how many groups you made.
Write how many in all.

1.

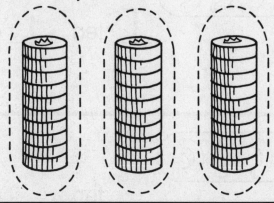

_3_ groups of 10

30
_____

2.

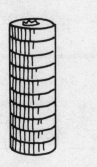 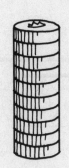

_____ groups of 10

_____

3.

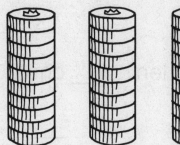 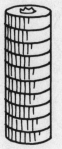 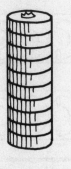 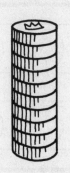

_____ groups of 10

_____

Number Sense

4. Which group has the greater number?
Ring it.

4 groups of 10

2 groups of 10

Tens and Ones to 20

Write how many.

1.
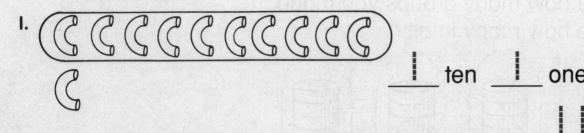

___|___ ten   ___|___ ones

___|_|___

2.
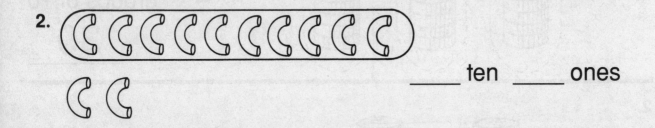

_____ ten   _____ ones

_____

3.
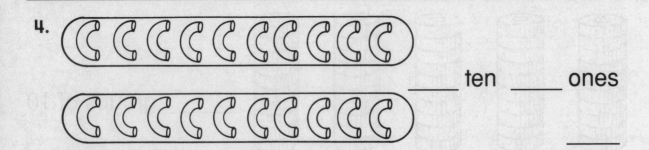

_____ ten   _____ ones

_____

4.

_____ ten   _____ ones

_____

Number Sense

5. How many red are there?
Ring the better estimate.

    more than 10   fewer than 10

Tens and Ones to 50

Count. Write how many in all.

1.

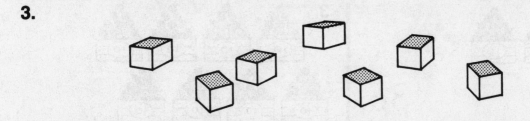

30

2.

3.

4.

Problem Solving

5. The game has 20 white cubes.
   It has 1 red cube.
   How many cubes does the
   game have in all?

   _____ cubes

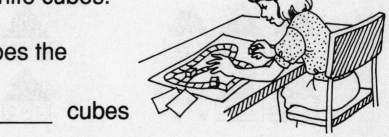

Tens and Ones to 80

Use place-value models.
Complete the table.

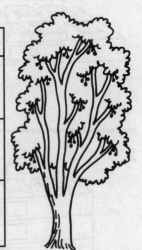

1.	Tens	Ones	In All
	6	5	65
	3	6	____
	5	4	____

Count. Write how many in all.

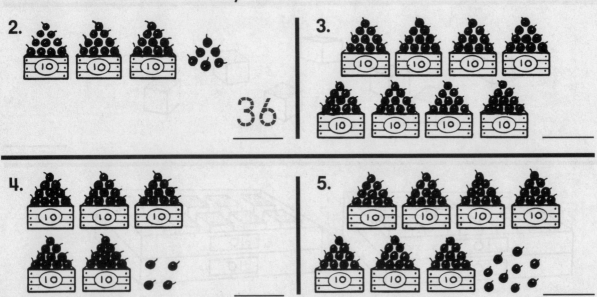

2. 36

3. ____

4. ____

5. ____

Number Sense

6. Ring the group that has the greater number.

68

Tens and Ones to 100

Use place-value models.
Complete the table.

1.

Tens	Ones	In All
7	4	74
8	4	
9	4	

Count. Write how many in all.

2.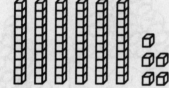

65

3.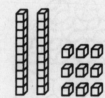

____

4.

____

5.

____

Number Sense

6. Ring the number that is less.

8 tens 6 ones   7 tens 6 ones

69

Problem-Solving Strategy

Use Estimation

Ring the best estimate.
Ring groups of 10 to check your estimate.

1.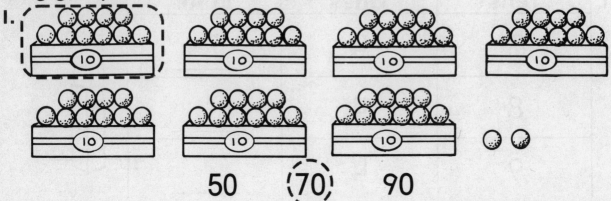

   50   (70)   90

2.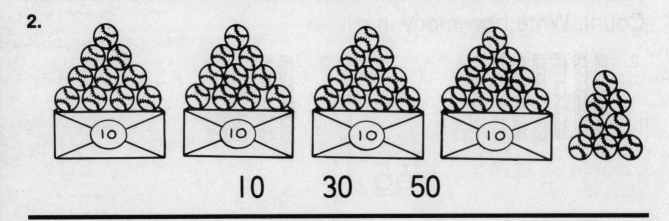

   10   30   50

3.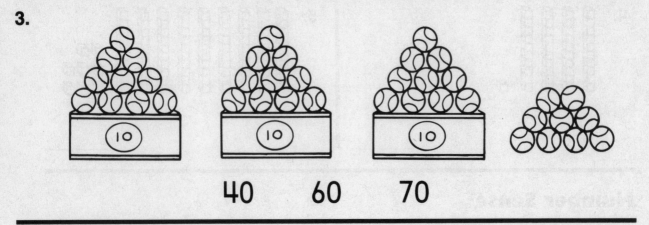

   40   60   70

Reasoning

Write the answer.

4. Is 57 closer to 50 or to 60? _____

70

Counting Pennies

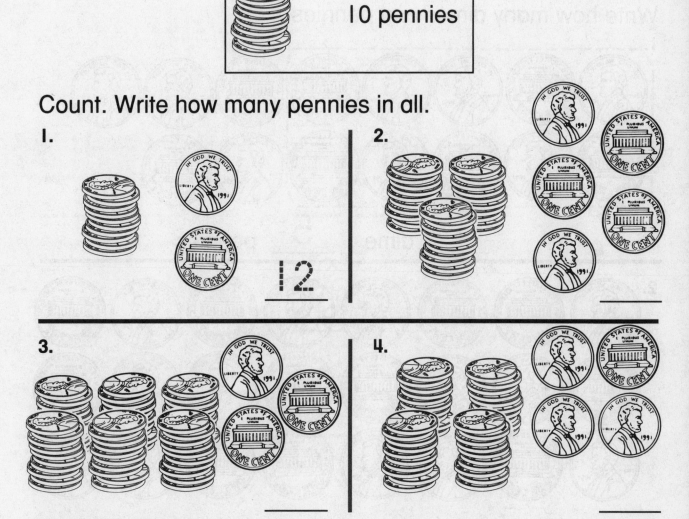	10 pennies

Count. Write how many pennies in all.

1.

_12_

2.

_____

3.

_____

4.

_____

Number Sense

5. Ring the greater amount of money.

Trading Groups

You will need 2 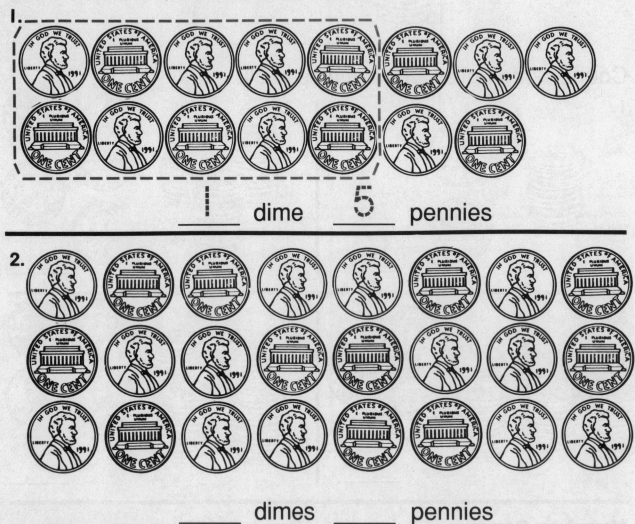.
Count the pennies. Ring groups of 10.
Put 1 dime on each group of 10.
Write how many dimes and pennies.

1.

____1____ dime   ____5____ pennies

2.

_____ dimes   _____ pennies

Reasoning

3. Which money is easier to count?

72

Comparing Numbers

Use place-value models.
Ring the number that is greater. Use 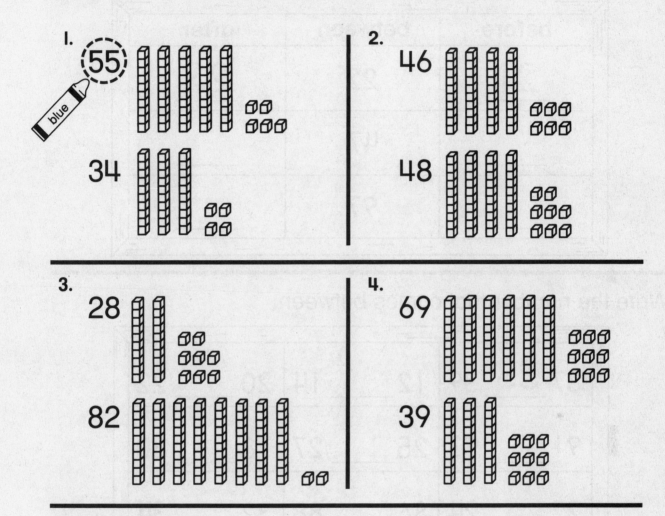 blue ✏.

1. (55)   34

2. 46   48

3. 28   82

4. 69   39

Number Sense

5. Which numbers are less than 50? Ring them in red ✏.

34   78   12   99   41   56   29   21

50

73   22   44   20   38   63   92   85

Before, After, Between

Use place-value models. Write the numbers.

1.

before	between	after
21	22	23
___	47	___
___	97	___

Write the number that comes between.

2.

37 **38** 39	12 ___ 14	20 ___ 22
91 ___ 93	25 ___ 27	78 ___ 80
22 ___ 24	86 ___ 88	32 ___ 34
61 ___ 63	44 ___ 46	80 ___ 82

Reasoning

Ring **Yes** or **No**.

3. Does 76 come before 77?   Yes   No

4. Is 76 less than 77?   Yes   No

Order to 100

Write the missing numbers.

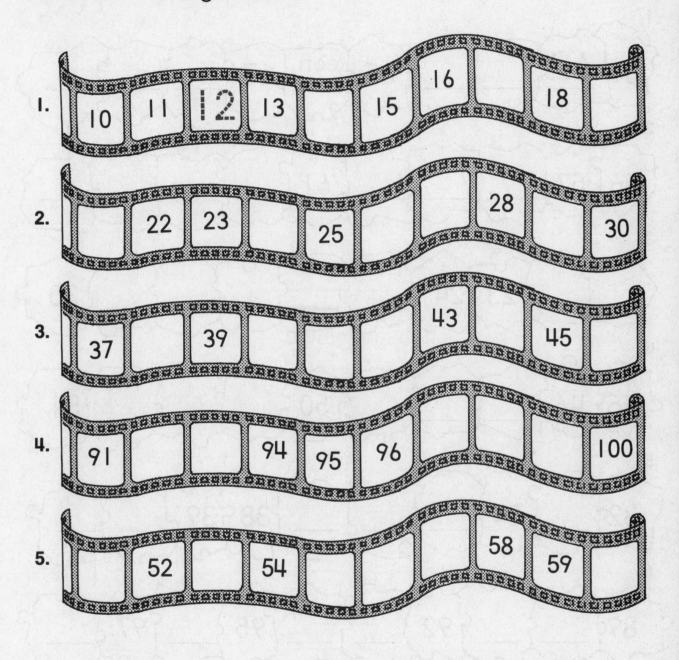

1. 10 11 12 13 ___ 15 16 ___ 18 ___

2. ___ 22 23 ___ 25 ___ ___ 28 ___ 30

3. 37 ___ 39 ___ ___ 43 ___ 45

4. 91 ___ ___ 94 95 96 ___ ___ 100

5. ___ 52 ___ 54 ___ ___ 58 59

Story Corner

Read this riddle. Write the numbers.

6. We are numbers between 81 and 86.
   We come after 83.

   _____ and _____

75

Numbers to 100

Write the missing numbers.

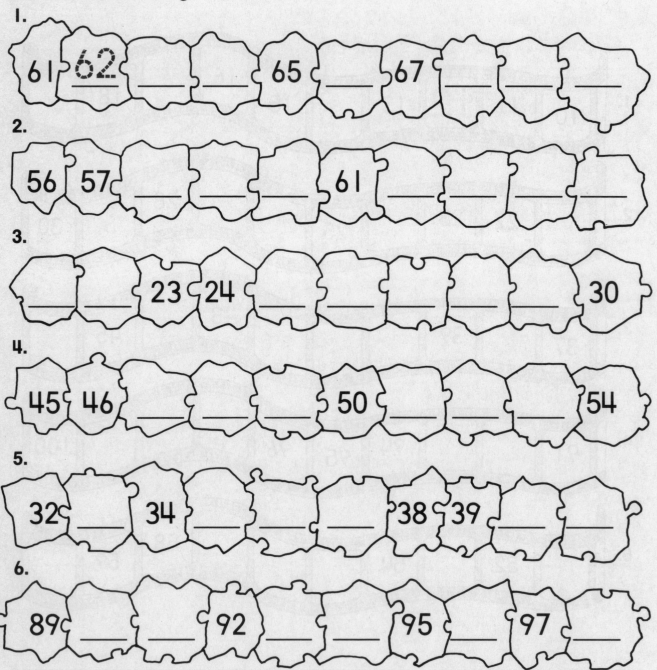

1. 61 | 62 | ___ | ___ | 65 | ___ | 67 | ___ | ___ | ___

2. 56 | 57 | ___ | ___ | ___ | 61 | ___ | ___ | ___ | ___

3. ___ | ___ | 23 | 24 | ___ | ___ | ___ | ___ | ___ | 30

4. 45 | 46 | ___ | ___ | ___ | 50 | ___ | ___ | ___ | 54

5. 32 | ___ | 34 | ___ | ___ | ___ | 38 | 39 | ___ | ___

6. 89 | ___ | ___ | 92 | ___ | ___ | 95 | ___ | 97 | ___

Number Sense

7. Ring the numbers that are less than 20.

15   16   17   18   19   20   21   22   23   24   25

76

Number Patterns

Use counters.

1. Stack 5 counters in each space.
   How many counters in all?

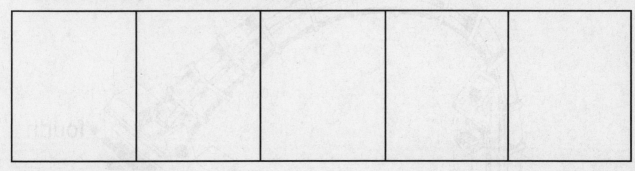

Count by fives.

_5_   _10_   ___   ___   ___

---

2. Stack 10 counters in each space. How many counters in all?

Count by tens.

_10_   ___   ___   ___   ___

Number Sense

3. Write the missing number.

| 11 | 21 | 31 | 41 | 51 | ___ |

Ordinal Numbers

Match.

1.

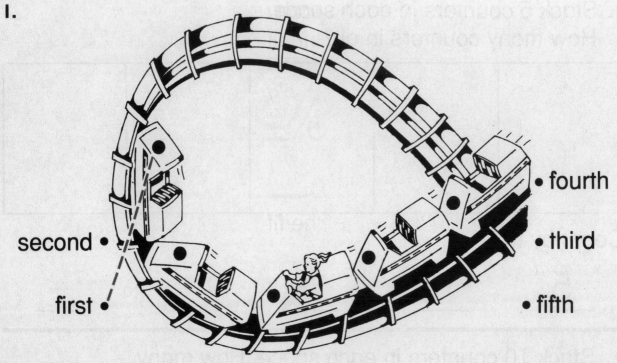

second •

first •

• fourth

• third

• fifth

2.

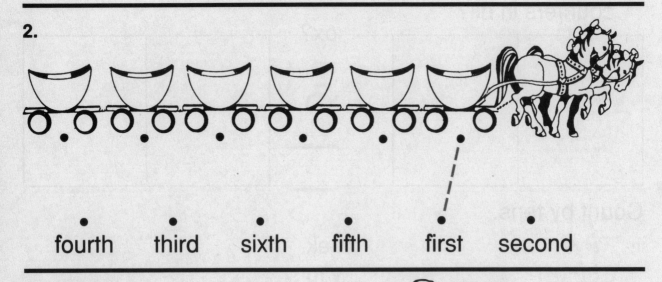

fourth   third   sixth   fifth   first   second

Reasoning

3. Which animal is first?
   Ring the answer.

rabbit   duck   can't tell

Problem-Solving Strategy

Use a Pattern

Look for a pattern to answer each question.

1. How many marbles are in the fifth and sixth boxes?

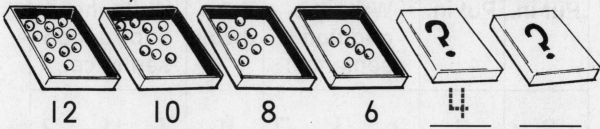

12   10   8   6   4   ___

---

2. How many marbles are in the fifth, sixth and seventh boxes?

5   10   15   20   ___   ___   ___

---

3. How many are in the last box?

20 25 30 35 40 45 ?

___

Story Corner

4. Fran saves dimes every week.
   She uses the pattern below to save.
   How many dimes should she save in Week 4?

Week	1	2	3	4
Dimes	1	3	5	___

Adding and Subtracting

Work with a friend. You need connecting cubes. Listen and do.

	Put in.	Put in.	Write the addition sentence.	Take away.	Write the subtraction sentence.
1.	3	4	$3 + 4 = 7$	4	$7 - 4 = 3$
2.	6	2		2	
3.	4	6		6	
4.	5	5		5	
5.	6	3		3	

Story Corner

6. Look at the picture.
   Make up a story problem.
   Tell it to a friend.
   Write the number sentence. _____ ◯ _____ = _____

Counting On

Ring the greater number. Count on to add.

⑦
+1
8   ⟨7,8⟩

2
+⑧
10   ⟨8,9,10⟩

⑧
+3
11   ⟨8,9,10,11⟩

Ring the greater number. Write each sum.
Use counters to check.

1. ⑥   3   3   8   7   3
   +2   +6   +7   +1   +2   +9
    8

2.   1   9   2   3   8   5
    +9   +2   +8   +5   +3   +2

3.   6   7   1   2   9   6
    +1   +3   +7   +9   +3   +3

Reasoning

4. There are 10 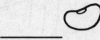 in all.
   How many are inside the bag?

   _____

Doubles

Ring each double. Write each sum.

1. (3 + 3) = 6   3 + 5 = ___   8 + 3 = ___

2. 4 + 2 = ___   6 + 6 = ___   4 + 4 = ___

3. 2 + 2 = ___   5 + 5 = ___   2 + 6 = ___

4.
$$\begin{array}{c}1\\+1\\\hline\end{array}\qquad\begin{array}{c}1\\+7\\\hline\end{array}\qquad\begin{array}{c}3\\+7\\\hline\end{array}\qquad\begin{array}{c}2\\+8\\\hline\end{array}\qquad\begin{array}{c}3\\+3\\\hline\end{array}\qquad\begin{array}{c}6\\+3\\\hline\end{array}$$

5.
$$\begin{array}{c}5\\+3\\\hline\end{array}\qquad\begin{array}{c}5\\+5\\\hline\end{array}\qquad\begin{array}{c}4\\+4\\\hline\end{array}\qquad\begin{array}{c}2\\+7\\\hline\end{array}\qquad\begin{array}{c}8\\+3\\\hline\end{array}\qquad\begin{array}{c}6\\+6\\\hline\end{array}$$

Problem Solving

Solve. Write the addition sentence.

6. The cow jumped over the moon 4 times.
   Then it jumped 4 more times.
   How many times did it jump in all?

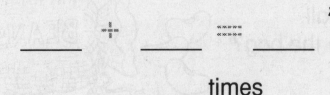

____ + ____ = ____

____ times

82

Doubles Plus One

Add.
Use counters if you
need to.

1.
$$5 \atop +5 = 10$$ $$5 \atop +6$$ $$2 \atop +3$$ $$1 \atop +1$$ $$4 \atop +4$$ $$1 \atop +2$$

2.
$$4 \atop +5$$ $$3 \atop +3$$ $$0 \atop +0$$ $$3 \atop +4$$ $$2 \atop +2$$ $$0 \atop +1$$

Number Sense

Do each one in your head.
Then write the sum.

3. $4 + 4 = 8$,

   so $4 + 5 = \underline{9}$

4. $0 + 0 = 0$,

   so $0 + 1 = \underline{}$

5. $2 + 2 = 4$,

   so $2 + 3 = \underline{}$

6. $1 + 1 = 2$,

   so $1 + 2 = \underline{}$

7. $5 + 5 = 10$,

   so $5 + 6 = \underline{}$

8. $3 + 3 = 6$,

   so $3 + 4 = \underline{}$

Order of Addends

7,8,9,10

$$7 + 3 = 10$$

$$3 + 7 = 10$$

I see 4 and 4. That makes 8, and 1 more makes 9.

$$5 + 4 = 9$$

$$4 + 5 = 9$$

Add.

1.
$$8 + 2 = $$
$$2 + 8 = $$
$$5 + 5 = $$
$$5 + 6 = $$
$$8 + 1 = $$
$$1 + 8 = $$

2.
$$3 + 3 = $$
$$9 + 3 = $$
$$4 + 4 = $$
$$3 + 9 = $$
$$9 + 2 = $$
$$2 + 9 = $$

Visual Thinking

3. Ring the correct answer.

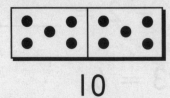

10

more than 10

less than 10

more than 10

less than 10

Problem-Solving Strategy

Make and Use a Bar Graph

Work with a group of ten friends. Ask which animal each friend in the group likes best. Use tally marks ||||| to count.

kitten ___ pony ___ puppy ___ bunny ___

Color a ☐ for each tally mark.

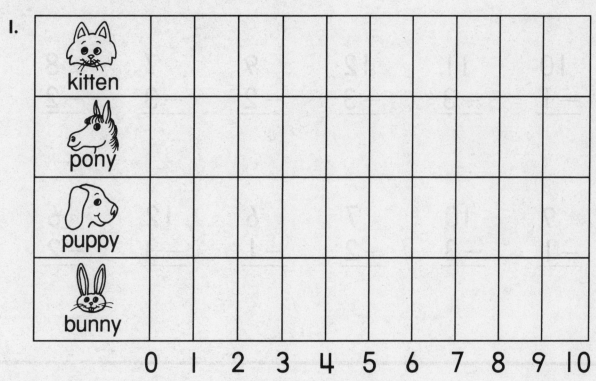

2. Which animal did your group like best? _____

3. How many in your group chose this animal? _____

4. Which animal did your group like the least? _____

Counting Back

$$10 \atop \underline{-1}$$ $\overparen{10,9}$ $\quad$ $$11 \atop \underline{-3}$$ $\overparen{11,10,9,8}$ $\quad$ $$10 \atop \underline{-2}$$ $\overparen{10,9,8}$

$$\;9$$ $\qquad\qquad\quad$ $$\;8$$ $\qquad\qquad\quad$ $$\;8$$

Count back to subtract.

1. $$11 \atop \underline{-2}$$ $$8 \atop \underline{-1}$$ $$9 \atop \underline{-3}$$ $$7 \atop \underline{-1}$$ $$8 \atop \underline{-3}$$ $$10 \atop \underline{-2}$$

2. $$10 \atop \underline{-1}$$ $$11 \atop \underline{-3}$$ $$12 \atop \underline{-3}$$ $$9 \atop \underline{-2}$$ $$7 \atop \underline{-3}$$ $$8 \atop \underline{-2}$$

3. $$9 \atop \underline{-1}$$ $$10 \atop \underline{-3}$$ $$7 \atop \underline{-2}$$ $$6 \atop \underline{-1}$$ $$12 \atop \underline{-3}$$ $$6 \atop \underline{-2}$$

Reasoning

4. Which has the greatest difference? Ring it.

$$50 \atop \underline{-3}$$ $\qquad$ $$50 \atop \underline{-2}$$ $\qquad$ $$50 \atop \underline{-1}$$

Counting Up

Count up to subtract.

1. $\begin{array}{r} 8 \\ -7 \\ \hline \end{array}$ 7, 8   (1 more)
    $\begin{array}{r} 11 \\ -8 \\ \hline \end{array}$ 8, 9, 10, 11   (3 more)
    $\begin{array}{r} 7 \\ -5 \\ \hline \end{array}$ 6, 7, 8   (2 more)
    $\begin{array}{r} 10 \\ -7 \\ \hline \end{array}$ 7, 8, 9, 10   (3 more)

2. $\begin{array}{r} 11 \\ -9 \\ \hline \end{array}$ (9, 10, 11)
    $\begin{array}{r} 10 \\ -8 \\ \hline \end{array}$ (8, 9, 10)
    $\begin{array}{r} 9 \\ -8 \\ \hline \end{array}$ (8, 9)
    $\begin{array}{r} 12 \\ -9 \\ \hline \end{array}$ (9, 10, 11, 12)

3. $\begin{array}{r} 10 \\ -9 \\ \hline \end{array}$
    $\begin{array}{r} 8 \\ -6 \\ \hline \end{array}$
    $\begin{array}{r} 6 \\ -5 \\ \hline \end{array}$
    $\begin{array}{r} 7 \\ -4 \\ \hline \end{array}$
    $\begin{array}{r} 9 \\ -7 \\ \hline \end{array}$
    $\begin{array}{r} 5 \\ -3 \\ \hline \end{array}$

4. $\begin{array}{r} 12 \\ -8 \\ \hline \end{array}$
    $\begin{array}{r} 5 \\ -2 \\ \hline \end{array}$
    $\begin{array}{r} 7 \\ -6 \\ \hline \end{array}$
    $\begin{array}{r} 10 \\ -8 \\ \hline \end{array}$
    $\begin{array}{r} 8 \\ -5 \\ \hline \end{array}$
    $\begin{array}{r} 6 \\ -4 \\ \hline \end{array}$

Reasoning

Use counting back or counting up to subtract.

5. $\begin{array}{r} 11 \\ -8 \\ \hline \end{array}$
    $\begin{array}{r} 12 \\ -3 \\ \hline \end{array}$
    $\begin{array}{r} 9 \\ -6 \\ \hline \end{array}$
    $\begin{array}{r} 10 \\ -2 \\ \hline \end{array}$
    $\begin{array}{r} 8 \\ -1 \\ \hline \end{array}$
    $\begin{array}{r} 8 \\ -6 \\ \hline \end{array}$

Ring in red the counting up facts.
Ring in blue the counting back facts.

Addition and Subtraction

Add. Then subtract.
Use counters to show.

1. $6 + 5 =$ __11__

    $11 - 5 =$ __6__

2. $7 + 4 =$ ___

    $11 - 4 =$ ___

3. $5 + 5 =$ ___

    $10 - 5 =$ ___

4. $8 + 4 =$ ___

    $12 - 4 =$ ___

5. $9 + 2 =$ ___

    $11 - 2 =$ ___

6. $6 + 6 =$ ___

    $12 - 6 =$ ___

7. $7 + 3 =$ ___

    $10 - 3 =$ ___

8. $7 + 5 =$ ___

    $12 - 5 =$ ___

Problem Solving

Ring **Add** or **Subtract**.

9. A pieman made 8 pies. Then he made
    4 more. How many did he make in all?

    Add   Subtract

Fact Families

Add or subtract. Ring the sentence
that does not belong.

1.

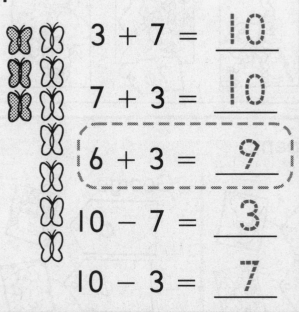

$3 + 7 = \underline{10}$

$7 + 3 = \underline{10}$

$\boxed{6 + 3 = \underline{9}}$

$10 - 7 = \underline{3}$

$10 - 3 = \underline{7}$

2.

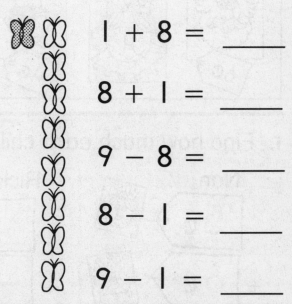

$1 + 8 = \underline{\hphantom{00}}$

$8 + 1 = \underline{\hphantom{00}}$

$9 - 8 = \underline{\hphantom{00}}$

$8 - 1 = \underline{\hphantom{00}}$

$9 - 1 = \underline{\hphantom{00}}$

3.

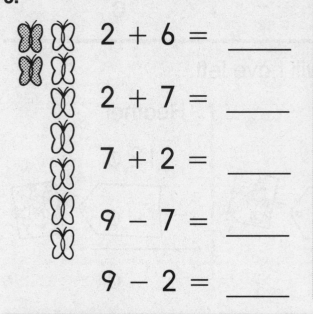

$2 + 6 = \underline{\hphantom{00}}$

$2 + 7 = \underline{\hphantom{00}}$

$7 + 2 = \underline{\hphantom{00}}$

$9 - 7 = \underline{\hphantom{00}}$

$9 - 2 = \underline{\hphantom{00}}$

4.

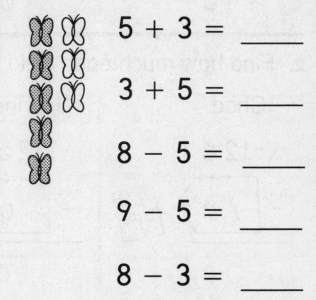

$5 + 3 = \underline{\hphantom{00}}$

$3 + 5 = \underline{\hphantom{00}}$

$8 - 5 = \underline{\hphantom{00}}$

$9 - 5 = \underline{\hphantom{00}}$

$8 - 3 = \underline{\hphantom{00}}$

Reasoning

5. Write the difference.

$13 - 5 = 8$, so $13 - 8 = \underline{\hphantom{00}}$

Using Pennies

1. Find how much each child spent.

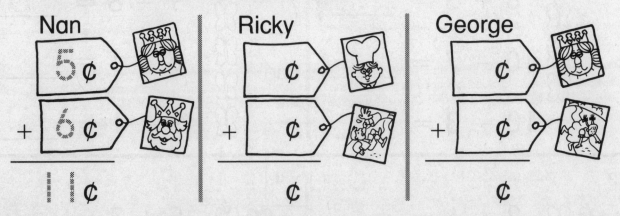

Nan	Ricky	George
5¢	¢	¢
+ 6¢	+ ¢	+ ¢
11¢	¢	¢

2. Find how much each child will have left.

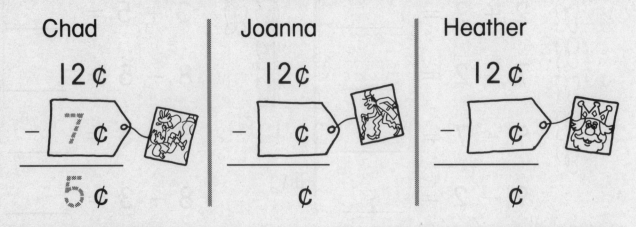

Chad	Joanna	Heather
12¢	12¢	12¢
− 7¢	− ¢	− ¢
5¢	¢	¢

Number Sense

3. Who spent the same amount of money?

_____ and _____

90

Probability

Possible or Impossible

You need △ △ △ ○ □ ⬜.

1. Put the shapes into the bag. Shake. Pick one.

   Color a □ to show your pick.

2. Make a prediction. If you pick 9 more times,
   which shape do you think you will pick most often?

   Ring your prediction.   △   ○   □

3. Put the shape back into the bag.
   Shake. Repeat 9 more times.

△										
○										
□										

0   1   2   3   4   5   6   7   8   9   10

4. Was your prediction right? Ring **Yes** or **No**.

   Yes   No

Visual Thinking

5. Ring the shape you picked least often.   △   ○   □

Problem Solving

Choose the Operation

Ring **Add** or **Subtract**.
Then write the number sentence.

1. Humpty Dumpty fell.
   9 men came.
   Then 3 more came.
   How many men came in all?

   (Add)   Subtract

   9 (+) 3 = 12

   12 men

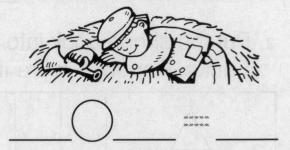

2. Little Boy Blue has 9 sheep.
   He has 5 cows.
   How many more sheep than
   cows does he have?

   Add   Subtract

   ___ ○ ___ = ___

   ___ more sheep

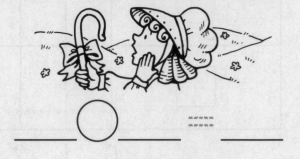

3. Little Bo-Peep had 11 sheep.
   She lost 3.
   How many sheep does she
   have left?

   Add   Subtract

   ___ ○ ___ = ___

   ___ sheep

Story Corner

4. Make up an addition or a subtraction
   story about the picture.
   Draw a picture to show the story.

Estimating and Comparing Length

You need crayons.

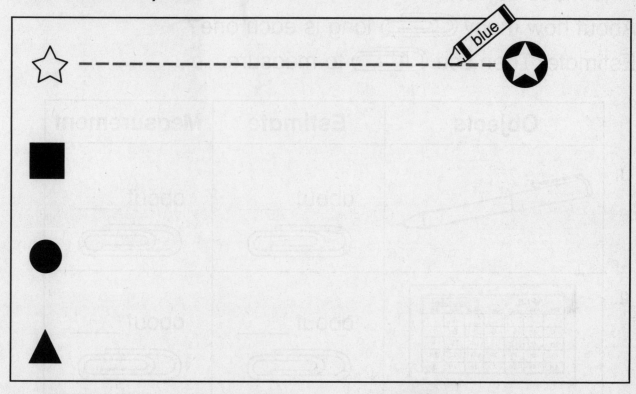

1. Start at ☆. Draw a blue line to the ★.

2. Start at ■. Draw a yellow line that is as long as the blue line.

3. Start at ●. Draw a red line that is longer than the blue line.

4. Start at ▲. Draw a green line that is shorter than the blue line.

Visual Thinking

5. Cross out the object that is longer than the pencil.

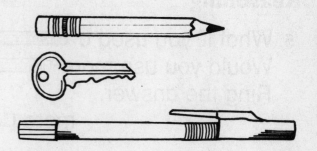

Measuring in Nonstandard Units

Find these objects.

About how many ⊂▭▭⊃ long is each one?

Estimate. Then use ⊂▭▭⊃ to measure.

	Objects	Estimate	Measurement
1.		about ____	about ____
2.	APRIL	about ____	about ____
3.		about ____	about ____
4.		about ____	about ____

Reasoning

5. What if you used a ✏️▭▭▭▶ to measure the objects? Would you use more ✏️▭▭▭▶ or more ⊂▭▭⊃? Ring the answer.

more ✏️▭▭▭▶   more ⊂▭▭⊃

Measuring in Inches

Use your inch ruler to measure.
Write how many inches tall.

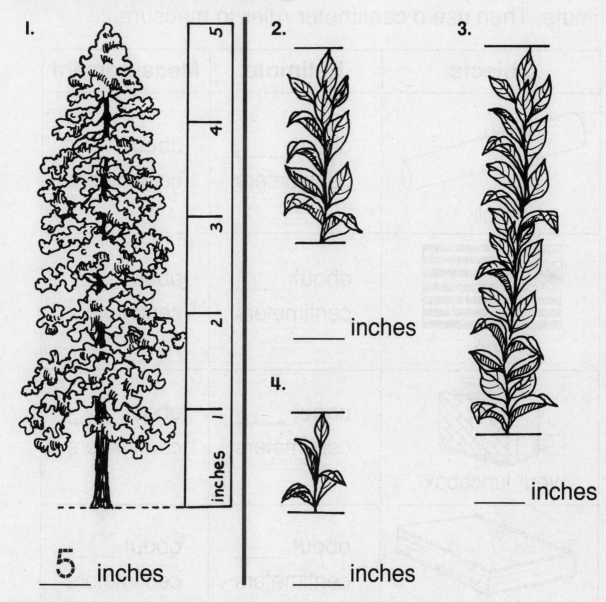

1.

5
4
3
2
1
inches

_5_ inches

2.

___ inches

4.

___ inches

3.

___ inches

Reasoning

5. What is the name of this shape?

6. Measure the sides.
What did you find out?

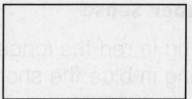

Measuring in Centimeters

Find these objects.
About how many centimeters long is each one?
Estimate. Then use a centimeter ruler to measure.

	Objects	Estimate	Measurement
1.	chalk	about ____ centimeters	about ____ centimeters
2.	flag	about ____ centimeters	about ____ centimeters
3.	your lunchbox	about ____ centimeters	about ____ centimeters
4.	book	about ____ centimeters	about ____ centimeters

Number Sense

5. Ring in red the longest object.
6. Ring in blue the shortest object.

More Measurement

Make a ruler.

Cut a strip of paper 10 centimeters long.

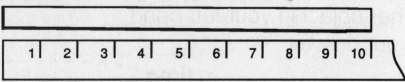

Draw an **X** to show your estimate.

Then use your ruler to check.

Draw a ✓ to show your measurement.

Objects	More than 10 centimeters	Less than 10 centimeters	About 10 centimeters
1. your arm	X ✓		
2. your shoe			
3. clock			
4. eraser			

Reasoning

5. 1 decimeter = 10 centimeters,

   so 2 decimeters = _____ centimeters.

Estimating and Measuring Weight

Which object in each pair is heavier?
Hold one object in your right hand.
Hold the other object in your left hand.
Then ring your answer.

1.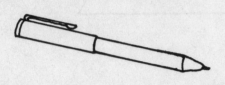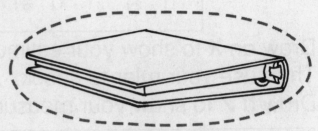

2.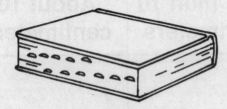

3.

4.

Reasoning

5. Ring the heaviest object.

cup   pan   block

Estimating Capacity

About how many lids full of rice does
each container hold?
You need these.

lid   rice   cup   milk carton   bowl   milk carton

Estimate. Then measure.

	Object	Estimate	Measurement
1.	cup	about _____ lids	about _____ lids
2.	milk carton	about _____ lids	about _____ lids
3.	bowl	about _____ lids	about _____ lids
4.	milk carton	about _____ lids	about _____ lids

Reasoning

5. Ring the one that holds more.

Estimating Temperature

Which one in each pair is hot?
Ring it.

1.

2.

3.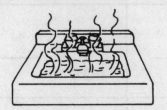

4.

Number Sense

Read the thermometers.
5. Ring the one that shows
   the hottest temperature.

Problem Solving
Write Appropriate Questions
Some children counted birds they saw at a feeder. Then they made this table.

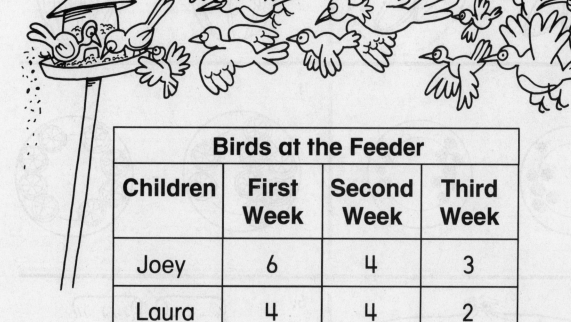

Birds at the Feeder			
Children	First Week	Second Week	Third Week
Joey	6	4	3
Laura	4	4	2
Khalid	5	2	4

1. Read the table. Write a question about the table.

_____

- -

_____

_____

- -

Story Corner
2. Write another question about the table.
   Have your friend give the answer.

Fair Shares

Ring the ones that show fair shares.

1.

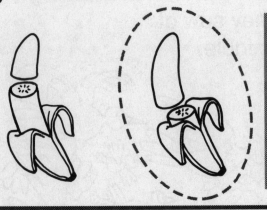

2.

3.

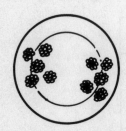 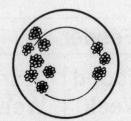

4.

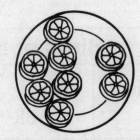 

5.

6.

 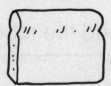

Visual Thinking

7. Rosa and Joey want fair shares of pizza.
How should the pizza be cut?
Draw a line to show.
Your pizza should show equal parts.

Halves

Draw a line to show two
equal parts. Then color to show $\frac{1}{2}$.

1.
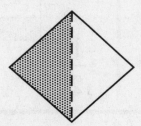

2.

3.
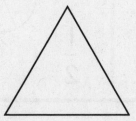

4.
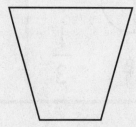

Find the shapes that show two equal parts. Color $\frac{1}{2}$.

5.
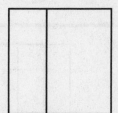  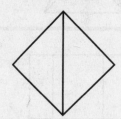

Problem Solving

Solve.

6. Two squirrels shared 4 nuts.
   Each had one half of the 4 nuts.
   How many nuts did each squirrel have?

   _____ nuts

Thirds

Ring the fraction that each shape shows.

1.

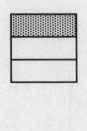
$\frac{1}{2}$ $\left(\frac{1}{3}\right)$

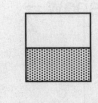
$\frac{1}{2}$ $\frac{1}{3}$

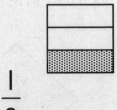
$\frac{1}{2}$ $\frac{1}{3}$

2.

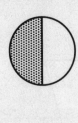
$\frac{1}{2}$ $\frac{1}{3}$

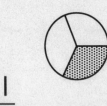
$\frac{1}{2}$ $\frac{1}{3}$

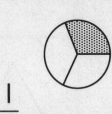
$\frac{1}{2}$ $\frac{1}{3}$

Find the shapes that show three equal parts. Color $\frac{1}{3}$.

3.

4.

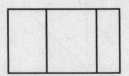

Visual Thinking

5. Which is greater, $\frac{1}{2}$ or $\frac{1}{3}$?

Ring the greater fraction.

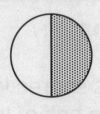

$\frac{1}{2}$ $\frac{1}{3}$

Fourths

Ring the fraction that each shape shows.

1.

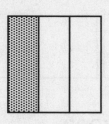

$\frac{1}{2}$ $\left(\frac{1}{3}\right)$ $\frac{1}{4}$

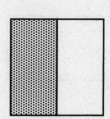

$\frac{1}{2}$ $\frac{1}{3}$ $\frac{1}{4}$

$\frac{1}{2}$ $\frac{1}{3}$ $\frac{1}{4}$

2.

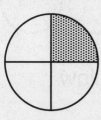

$\frac{1}{2}$ $\frac{1}{3}$ $\frac{1}{4}$

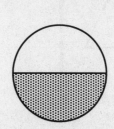

$\frac{1}{2}$ $\frac{1}{3}$ $\frac{1}{4}$

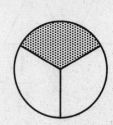

$\frac{1}{2}$ $\frac{1}{3}$ $\frac{1}{4}$

Find the shapes that show four equal parts. Color $\frac{1}{4}$.

3.

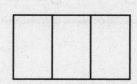

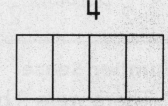

Visual Thinking

4. Which is greater, $\frac{1}{3}$ or $\frac{1}{4}$?

Ring the greater fraction.

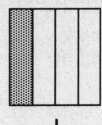

$\frac{1}{4}$

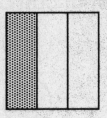

$\frac{1}{3}$

Fractions in Groups

Color to show each fraction

1.
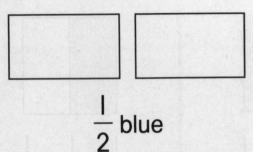

$\frac{1}{2}$ blue

2.
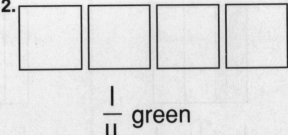

$\frac{1}{4}$ green

3.
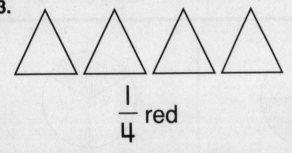

$\frac{1}{4}$ red

4.
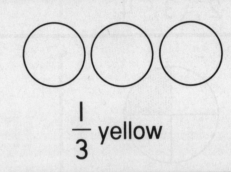

$\frac{1}{3}$ yellow

5.
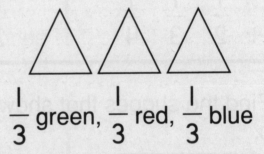

$\frac{1}{2}$ purple, $\frac{1}{2}$ orange

6.

$\frac{1}{3}$ green, $\frac{1}{3}$ red, $\frac{1}{3}$ blue

Number Sense

7. There were 3 bears in all.
Write the fraction that tells
what part of the group is left.

 is left.

Problem Solving

Visualize the Results

What is missing from each circle on the right?
Find the missing part. Draw lines to match.

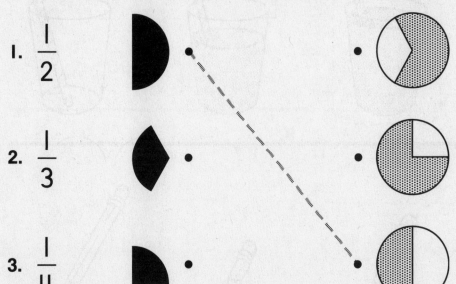

1. $\dfrac{1}{2}$

2. $\dfrac{1}{3}$

3. $\dfrac{1}{4}$

How does the rest of each picture look?
Draw the missing part to complete.

4.

$\dfrac{1}{2}$ a triangle

5.

$\dfrac{1}{3}$ a pie

Number Sense

6. There were 3 fair shares.
    Ring the fraction that tells what
    part of the pizza has been eaten.

$\dfrac{1}{2}$ $\dfrac{2}{3}$

Ordering Events

Ring in green what happened first.
Ring in red what happened last.

1.

  green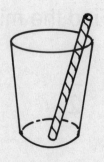

2.

3.

 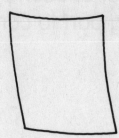

Story Corner

4. Make up a story about the pictures.
Share your story with a friend.

Estimating Time

Which takes more time to complete?
Ring it.

1.

2.

Which takes less time? Ring it.

3.

4.

Number Sense

5. Which takes the most time? Ring it.

Reading the Clock

Show each time on your .
Trace the hour hand on each clock.
Write the time.

1.

__3__ o'clock

2.

_____ o'clock

3.

_____ o'clock

Show each time on your .

Trace the minute hand on each clock.

Write the time.

4.

_____ o'clock

5.

_____ o'clock

6.

_____ o'clock

Problem Solving

Use your .

7. Travis's clock showed 4 o'clock.
Lee moved the short hand to the next hour.
Then Nell moved the short hand to the next hour.
What time does the clock show now?

_____ o'clock

Hour

Draw the hour hand so that both clocks show the same time.

1.

Write the time on the clock so that both clocks show the same time.

2.

Number Sense

3. Write the time on the clock so that it shows 1 hour later than 11 o'clock.

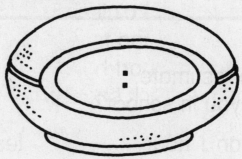

Exploring Minutes

Work with a friend.

Ring in orange your estimates.

Use your ⊕ or ⧗ to time each other.

Ring in green to show how much time passed.

1.

Write your name 1 time.

more than 1 minute

less than 1 minute

2.

"This story is about . . ."

Tell a long story.

more than 1 minute

less than 1 minute

3.

"99, 98, 97, . . ."

Count backward from 99 to 1.

more than 1 minute

less than 1 minute

Number Sense

4. Ring the better estimate.
   How long are you in school?

more than 1 hour   less than 1 hour

112

Thirty Minutes

Write each time.

1.

8:00 | : | :

2.

: | : | :

Show the time. Draw the minute hand.

3.

10:00 | 10:30 | 11:00

Number Sense

4. Ring the better estimate.
   How long will the movie last?

   more than 30 minutes

   less than 30 minutes

The Calendar

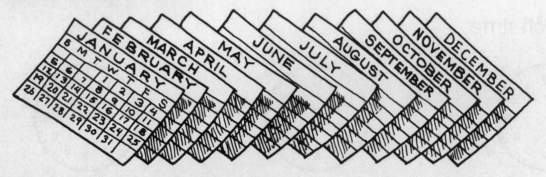

Complete the calendar for next month.

_____ , 20 _____

Sunday	Monday	Tuesday	Wednesday	Thursday	Friday	Saturday

Use the calendar. Write the answers.

1. How many days are in this month? _____ days

2. Name the first day of this month. _____

3. Name the last day of this month. _____

4. What day is today's date? _____

Number Sense

5. Look at calendars for this month and next month. Ring the answer.

Next month is _?_.

longer
shorter   same length

114

Problem-Solving Strategy

Use a Model

Use your to solve each problem.

Draw the hands on the clocks to show the times.

1.

   Brenda started her picture at 3:00. She finished 1 hour later. At what time did she finish?

2.

   George started eating lunch at 12:00. He finished 30 minutes later. At what time did he finish?

3.

   The music started at 8:00. It lasted 2 hours. At what time did it end?

Story Corner

4. Make up a story about the pictures. Share your story with a friend.

Penny and Nickel

Ring how much money is needed.

1.

2.

3.

Count by fives. Ring how much money is needed.

4.

Reasoning

Ring the one that costs less.

5.

6.

116

Dime

Count by fives and tens.
Ring how much money is needed.

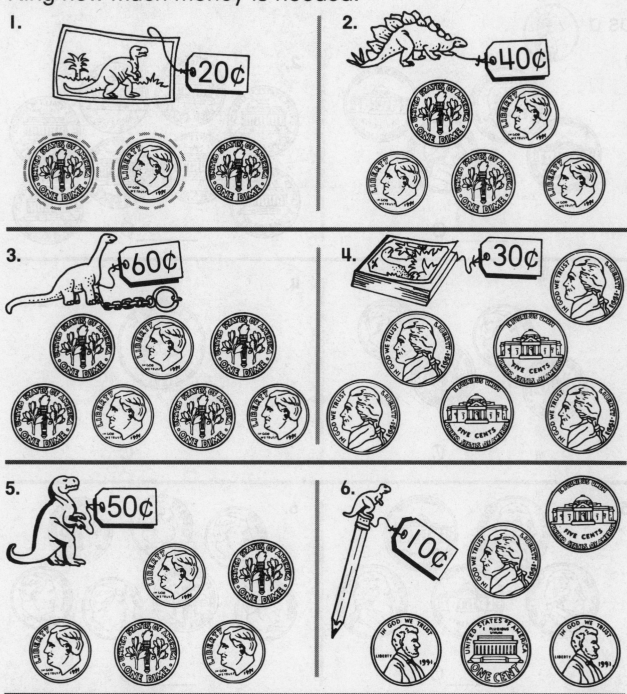

1. 20¢

2. 40¢

3. 60¢

4. 30¢

5. 50¢

6. 10¢

Number Sense

7. Ring the greatest amount.

20 pennies   4 dimes   5 nickels

Quarter

Write each amount.
Then ring the ones that have the same value as a .

1.

20 ¢

2.

_____ ¢

3.

_____ ¢

4.

_____ ¢

5.

_____ ¢

6.

_____ ¢

Reasoning

7. Ring the amount that you can show
   with the least number of coins.   15¢   20¢   25¢

Counting On from Nickels and Dimes

How much money? Count on.
Write the amount. Use punch-out coins.

1.

10 ¢   20 ¢   30 ¢   31 ¢   32 ¢ | 32 | ¢

2.

___ ¢   ___ ¢   ___ ¢   ___ ¢   ___ ¢   [   ] ¢

Write the amount.

3.

_____ ¢

4.

_____ ¢

Number Sense

5. Ring the greater amount.

2 dimes 9 pennies   4 nickels 8 pennies

Counting On from a Quarter

How much money? Count on from 25¢.
Write the amount. Use punch-out coins.

1. 25 ¢   30 ¢   35 ¢   36 ¢   37 ¢   37 ¢

2. ___ ¢   ___ ¢   ___ ¢   ___ ¢   ___ ¢

3. ___ ¢   ___ ¢   ___ ¢   ___ ¢   ___ ¢   ___ ¢

4. ___ ¢   ___ ¢   ___ ¢   ___ ¢   ___ ¢   ___ ¢   ___ ¢

Number Sense

5. Ring the coins to make 50¢.

Equal Amounts

Use your punch-out coins. Show a different way to make the same amount. Draw the coins you used. Write the value on each coin.

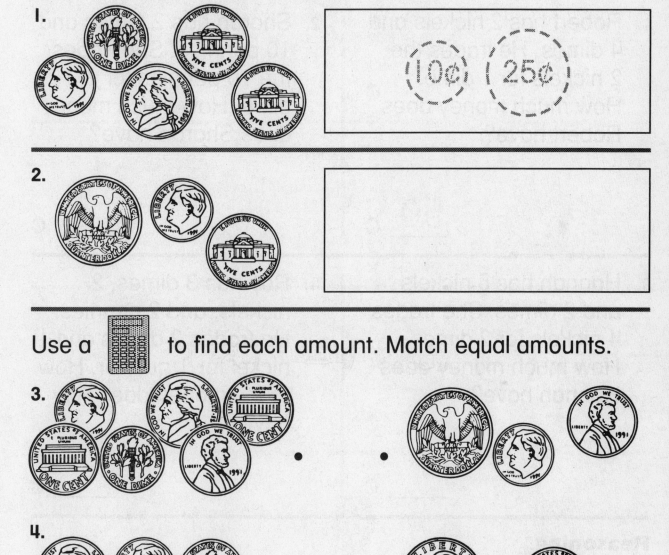

1.

2.

Use a [calculator] to find each amount. Match equal amounts.

3.

4.

Number Sense

5. Ring **Yes** or **No**. Can you show 20¢ with 3 coins?

Yes   No

Problem-Solving Strategy

Make a Model

Solve each problem. Act it out with a friend.
Use punch-out coins. Write the amount.

1. Robert has 2 nickels and 4 dimes. He trades the 2 nickels for 1 dime. How much money does Robert have?

 50 ¢

2. Sharon has 2 dimes and 10 pennies. She trades the 10 pennies for 1 dime. How much money does Sharon have?

_____ ¢

---

3. Hannah has 5 nickels and 2 dimes. She trades 4 nickels for 2 dimes. How much money does Hannah have?

_____ ¢

4. Roy has 3 dimes, 2 nickels, and 2 pennies. He trades 2 dimes and 1 nickel for 1 quarter. How much money does Roy have?

_____ ¢

Reasoning

5. You want to have fewer coins. Ring the coins you would give and take in a trade.

Give	Take
dime dime dime dime	quarter quarter dime
dime nickel nickel nickel	nickel penny penny
	penny penny penny

Adding and Subtracting

Do these in your head. Complete each table. Look for a pattern.

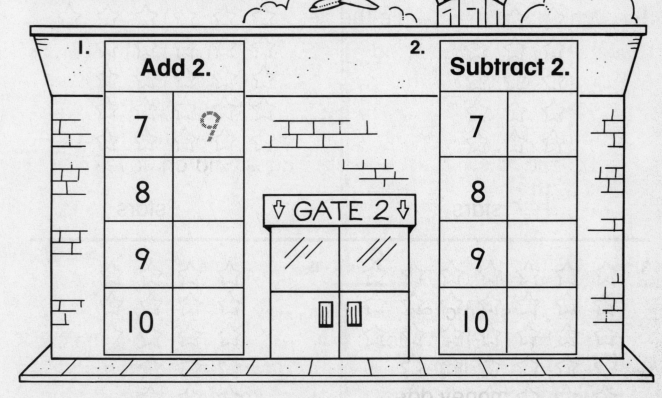

1. Add 2.

7	9
8	
9	
10	

2. Subtract 2.

7	
8	
9	
10	

GATE 2

Match the pairs that have the same sum.

3. 2 + 6 •   • 7 + 3

    3 + 7 •   • 5 + 2

    2 + 5 •   • 6 + 2

4. 0 + 8 •   • 6 + 3

    2 + 8 •   • 8 + 0

    3 + 6 •   • 8 + 2

Reasoning

Ring the answer.

5. Since $8 + 3 = 11$,
   then $7 + ? = 11$.

   4   5   6

6. Since $8 + 4 = 12$,
   then $7 + ? = 12$.

   3   4   5

Tens and Ones

Ring groups of ten.
Write how many stars in all.

1.

_____14_____ stars

2.

_____ stars

3.

_____ stars

4.

_____ stars

Number Sense • Estimation

About how many strawberries are in each bag?
Ring the better estimate.

5.

more than 30

fewer than 30

6.

between 40 and 60

between 10 and 30

Adding Tens

Add tens. Write each addition sentence.

1.

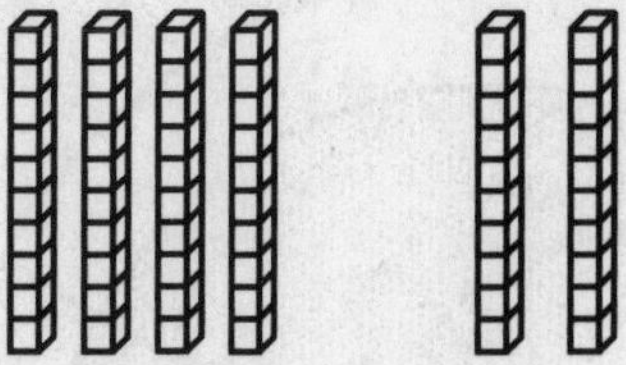

$\underline{40} + \underline{20} = \underline{60}$

2.

___ + ___ = ___

3.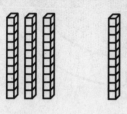

___ + ___ = ___

4.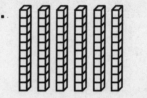

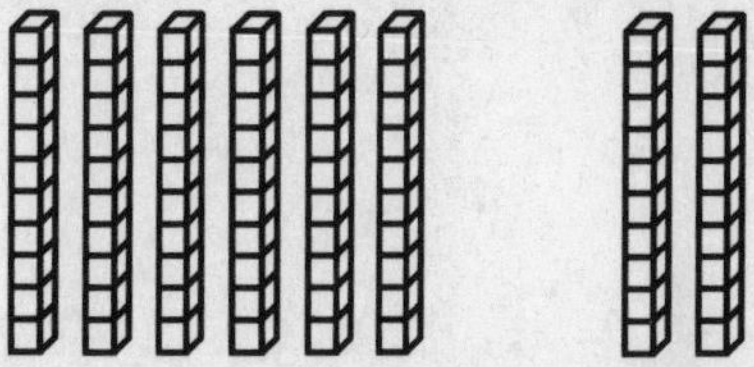

___ + ___ = ___

5.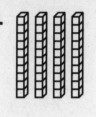

___ + ___ = ___

6.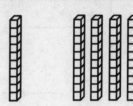

___ + ___ = ___

Number Sense

Do these in your head. Match the pairs to their sums.

7. $7 + 1$ •   • 30

$20 + 10$ •   • 6

$2 + 4$ •   • 8

8. $40 + 30$ •   • 40

$20 + 20$ •   • 9

$5 + 4$ •   • 70

Exploring 2-Digit Addition

Use a pencil and a paper clip to
make a spinner.
Spin the paper clip.
Write the number in the box.
Add. Write the sum.
Use punch-out tens and
ones if you need to.

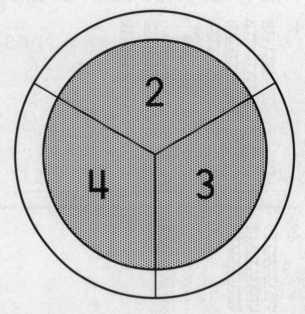

1. 54 + 3 = 57

2. 91 + ☐ = ___

3. 65 + ☐ = ___

4. 32 + ☐ = ___

5. 73 + ☐ = ___

6. 40 + ☐ = ___

7. 81 + ☐ = ___

8. 24 + ☐ = ___

9. 50 + ☐ = ___

10. 62 + ☐ = ___

Story Corner

Solve the riddle.

11. I am 1 more than 3 tens
    and 6 ones.
    What number am I?

    ___

12. I am 2 more than 4 tens
    and 5 ones.
    What number am I?

    ___

Adding 2-Digit Numbers

Add.

1.

tens	ones
5	8
+ 1	1
6	9

tens	ones
2	5
+ 2	3

tens	ones
4	3
+	2

tens	ones
1	2
+ 7	5

2.
$$66 \atop +13$$ $$32 \atop + \ 4$$ $$71 \atop +24$$ $$27 \atop +60$$ $$54 \atop +43$$

Number Sense

Solve the first problem. Then ring the better estimate for each problem. Use tens and ones models to check your estimate.

3.
$$40 \atop +40$$

$$40 \atop +51$$

more than 80

less than 80

$$36 \atop +32$$

more than 80

less than 80

4.
$$10 \atop +10$$

$$15 \atop + \ 2$$

more than 20

less than 20

$$23 \atop +14$$

more than 20

less than 20

Subtracting Tens

Add or subtract.

1.
70	50	80	60	40
+ 10	+ 20	− 30	− 20	+ 30
80				

2.
80	60	70	40	50
− 20	− 40	+ 20	− 20	+ 40

3.
80	60	70	60	80
+ 10	+ 30	− 40	− 30	− 10

Number Sense

Do these in your head. Look for a pattern.

4.
43	53	63	73	83
+ 10	+ 10	+ 10	+ 10	+ 10

5.
43	53	63	73	83
− 10	− 10	− 10	− 10	− 10

Exploring 2-Digit Subtraction

Use a pencil and a paper clip
to make a spinner.
Spin the paper clip.
Write the number in the box.
Subtract.
Write how many are left.
Use punch-out tens and
ones if you need to.

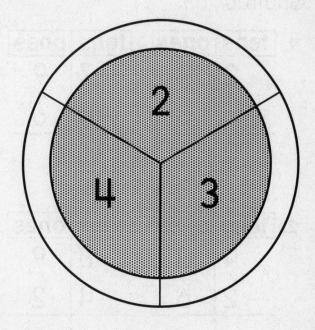

1. $45 - \boxed{4} = \underline{41}$

2. $28 - \boxed{} = \underline{}$

3. $89 - \boxed{} = \underline{}$

4. $66 - \boxed{} = \underline{}$

5. $37 - \boxed{} = \underline{}$

6. $55 - \boxed{} = \underline{}$

7. $76 - \boxed{} = \underline{}$

8. $48 - \boxed{} = \underline{}$

9. $85 - \boxed{} = \underline{}$

10. $39 - \boxed{} = \underline{}$

Story Corner

Solve the riddle.

11. I am 1 less than 5 tens
    and 3 ones. What
    number am I?

    _____

12. I am 2 less than 6 tens
    and 7 ones. What
    number am I?

    _____

Subtracting 2-Digit Numbers

Subtract.

1.

tens	ones
2	4
−	3
2	1

tens	ones
7	9
−4	6

tens	ones
5	5
−5	2

tens	ones
6	6
−5	2

2.

tens	ones
4	8
−2	6

tens	ones
8	9
−4	2

tens	ones
3	5
−1	3

tens	ones
2	7
−1	4

3.
$$70 - 30 \qquad 33 - 12 \qquad 96 - 33 \qquad 49 - 35 \qquad 55 - 23$$

Number Sense

Solve the first problem. Then ring the better
estimate for each problem. Use tens and ones
models to check your estimate.

4.
$$60 - 20$$

$$60 - 30$$

more than 40

less than 40

$$60 - 10$$

more than 40

less than 40

Adding and Subtracting

Add or subtract.
Color.

20 to 30	40 to 50	60 to 70	80 to 90
red	yellow	blue	brown

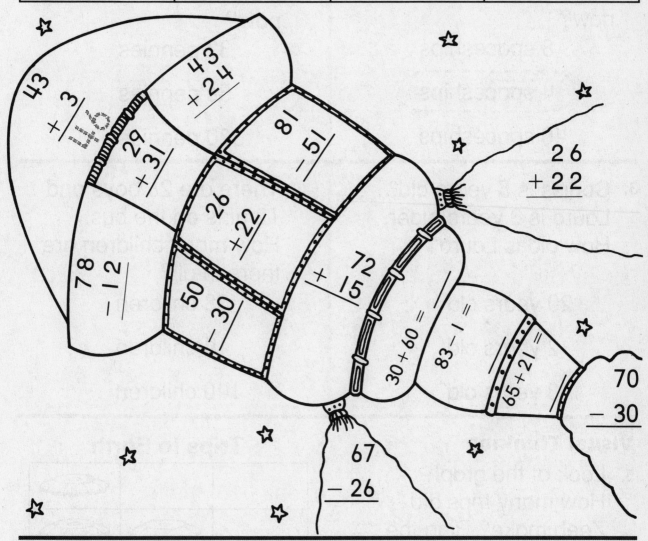

Number Sense

Ring the one you think will have the
greatest sum or difference.

1. $\begin{array}{r} 65 \\ +23 \end{array}$ $\begin{array}{r} 35 \\ +23 \end{array}$ $\begin{array}{r} 15 \\ +23 \end{array}$

2. $\begin{array}{r} 67 \\ -15 \end{array}$ $\begin{array}{r} 67 \\ -25 \end{array}$ $\begin{array}{r} 67 \\ -\ 5 \end{array}$

131

Problem Solving

Find the Reasonable Answer

Ring the answer that makes sense.

1. Miguel had 6 spaceships.
   He lost 2.
   How many does he have now?

   8 spaceships

   (4 spaceships)

   40 spaceships

2. Pete had 44 pennies.
   He gave Sue 12.
   How many does he have now?

   32 pennies

   56 pennies

   320 pennies

3. Corliss is 5 years old.
   Laura is 3 years older.
   How old is Laura?

   20 years old

   2 years old

   8 years old

4. There are 26 boys and 12 girls on the bus.
   How many children are there in all?

   38 children

   14 children

   140 children

Visual Thinking

5. Look at the graph.
   How many trips did Zeeb make? Ring the answer that makes sense.

   2 trips

   30 trips

   300 trips

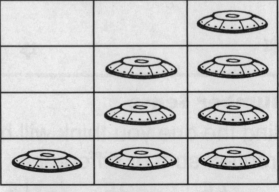

Trips to Earth

Jath   Zeeb   Lork

1 🛸 means 10 trips.

Problem-Solving Strategy

Use Estimation

Ring the better estimate.
Then find the exact answer.
You may use a .

1. Ben buys these things.

    32¢

   53¢

   About how much money

   did Ben spend?

   about 70¢

   (about 80¢)

   Exact answer _85_ ¢

2. Jen has 78¢.

   She buys for 55¢.

   About how much money

   does Jen have left?

   about 20¢

   about 30¢

   Exact answer ____ ¢

3. Len has 96¢.

   He buys a 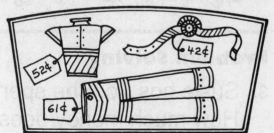 for 62¢.

   About how much money

   does Len have left?

   about 50¢

   about 30¢

   Exact answer ____ ¢

Story Corner

4. Make up a story problem about
   this picture. Give it to a friend
   to solve.

Sums and Differences

Tell a story about the pennies.
Add or subtract.

1.

 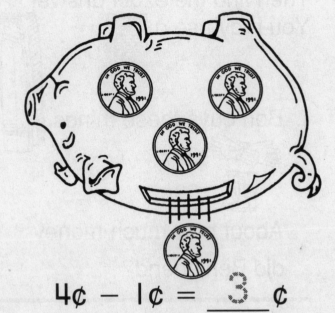

3¢ + 1¢ = ___4___ ¢   4¢ − 1¢ = ___3___ ¢

2.

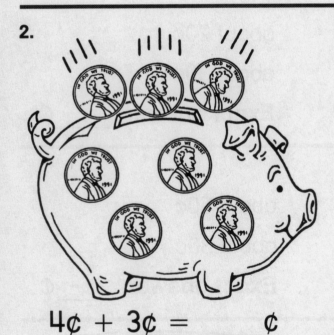 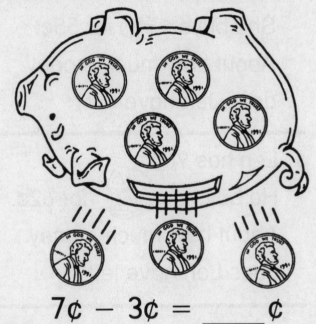

4¢ + 3¢ = _____ ¢   7¢ − 3¢ = _____ ¢

Problem Solving

3. Susie has 9¢. She spends 2¢.
How much money does she have left? _____ ¢

Using Doubles

Add or subtract. Use counters.

1.
$$\begin{array}{r} 1 \\ +\ 1 \\ \hline 2 \end{array} \qquad \begin{array}{r} 2 \\ -\ 1 \\ \hline 1 \end{array} \qquad\qquad \begin{array}{r} 2 \\ +\ 2 \\ \hline \end{array} \qquad \begin{array}{r} 4 \\ -\ 2 \\ \hline \end{array} \qquad\qquad \begin{array}{r} 3 \\ +\ 3 \\ \hline \end{array} \qquad \begin{array}{r} 6 \\ -\ 3 \\ \hline \end{array}$$

2.
$$\begin{array}{r} 4 \\ +\ 4 \\ \hline \end{array} \qquad \begin{array}{r} 8 \\ -\ 4 \\ \hline \end{array} \qquad\qquad \begin{array}{r} 5 \\ +\ 5 \\ \hline \end{array} \qquad \begin{array}{r} 10 \\ -\ 5 \\ \hline \end{array} \qquad\qquad \begin{array}{r} 6 \\ +\ 6 \\ \hline \end{array} \qquad \begin{array}{r} 12 \\ -\ 6 \\ \hline \end{array}$$

Number Sense
Try these in your head.

3.
$$\begin{array}{r} 7 \\ +\ 7 \\ \hline \end{array} \qquad \begin{array}{r} 14 \\ -\ 7 \\ \hline \end{array} \qquad\qquad \begin{array}{r} 8 \\ +\ 8 \\ \hline \end{array} \qquad \begin{array}{r} 16 \\ -\ 8 \\ \hline \end{array} \qquad\qquad \begin{array}{r} 9 \\ +\ 9 \\ \hline \end{array} \qquad \begin{array}{r} 18 \\ -\ 9 \\ \hline \end{array}$$

Doubles Plus One

Do these in your head. Then write the sums.

1. $1 + 1 = 2$, so $1 + 2 = \underline{3}$.

2. $4 + 4 = 8$, so $4 + 5 = \underline{}$.

3. $0 + 0 = 0$, so $0 + 1 = \underline{}$.

Write the sums.

4. $8 + 8 = \underline{}$, so $8 + 9 = \underline{}$.

5. $7 + 7 = \underline{}$, so $7 + 8 = \underline{}$.

Look for doubles to find the sums.

6.
$$\begin{array}{r} 5 \\ + 5 \\ \hline \end{array} \qquad \begin{array}{r} 3 \\ + 3 \\ \hline \end{array} \qquad \begin{array}{r} 6 \\ + 7 \\ \hline \end{array} \qquad \begin{array}{r} 4 \\ + 5 \\ \hline \end{array} \qquad \begin{array}{r} 2 \\ + 2 \\ \hline \end{array} \qquad \begin{array}{r} 3 \\ + 4 \\ \hline \end{array}$$

7.
$$\begin{array}{r} 2 \\ + 3 \\ \hline \end{array} \qquad \begin{array}{r} 8 \\ + 8 \\ \hline \end{array} \qquad \begin{array}{r} 5 \\ + 6 \\ \hline \end{array} \qquad \begin{array}{r} 8 \\ + 9 \\ \hline \end{array} \qquad \begin{array}{r} 4 \\ + 4 \\ \hline \end{array} \qquad \begin{array}{r} 6 \\ + 6 \\ \hline \end{array}$$

Reasoning

Write the sums.

8. $5 + 5 = 10$,

so $5 + 6 = \underline{}$.

9. $6 + 6 = 12$,

so $6 + 7 = \underline{}$.

Doubles Minus One

Do these in your head. Then write the sums.

1. $4 + 4 = 8$, so $4 + 3 = $ ___7___ .

2. $7 + 7 = 14$, so $7 + 6 = $ ____ .

3. $8 + 8 = 16$, so $8 + 7 = $ ____ .

4. $9 + 9 = 18$, so $9 + 8 = $ ____ .

5. $6 + 6 = 12$, so $6 + 5 = $ ____ .

Look for doubles to find the sums.

6.
$$\begin{array}{cccccc} 9 & 7 & 4 & 1 & 9 & 7 \\ +9 & +6 & +3 & +1 & +8 & +7 \\ \hline \end{array}$$

7.
$$\begin{array}{cccccc} 8 & 1 & 5 & 8 & 4 & 5 \\ +8 & +0 & +4 & +7 & +4 & +5 \\ \hline \end{array}$$

Number Sense

8. Ring $5 + 5$ | red | .

   Ring $5 + 4$ | blue | .

   Ring $5 + 6$ | green | .

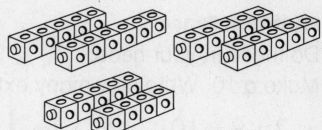

Make a 10

Use counters and the 10-frame.
Start with the greater number. Make a 10. Then add.

1.
$$7 + 4 = \underline{}$$ $$8 + 6$$ $$3 + 9$$ $$4 + 8$$ $$5 + 9$$ $$9 + 4$$

2.
$$9 + 6$$ $$3 + 8$$ $$7 + 5$$ $$2 + 9$$ $$5 + 8$$ $$9 + 7$$

3.
$$6 + 8$$ $$4 + 9$$ $$7 + 9$$ $$4 + 7$$ $$8 + 3$$ $$5 + 7$$

Number Sense

Do these in your head.
Make a 10. Write how many extra.

4. $2 + 9 = 10 + \underline{}$ extra | 5. $7 + 5 = 10 + \underline{}$ extra

Adding Three Numbers

Use a spinner.
Spin. Write the number in the box.

1.
$$\begin{array}{r} 2 \\ 2 \\ +\ \square \\ \hline \end{array} \qquad \begin{array}{r} 6 \\ 4 \\ +\ \square \\ \hline \end{array} \qquad \begin{array}{r} 5 \\ 5 \\ +\ \square \\ \hline \end{array}$$

2.
$$\begin{array}{r} 3 \\ 7 \\ +\ \square \\ \hline \end{array} \qquad \begin{array}{r} 4 \\ 4 \\ +\ \square \\ \hline \end{array} \qquad \begin{array}{r} 1 \\ 9 \\ +\ \square \\ \hline \end{array}$$

3.
$$\begin{array}{r} 2 \\ 8 \\ +\ \square \\ \hline \end{array} \quad \begin{array}{r} 1 \\ 1 \\ +\ \square \\ \hline \end{array} \quad \begin{array}{r} 8 \\ 2 \\ +\ \square \\ \hline \end{array} \quad \begin{array}{r} 3 \\ 3 \\ +\ \square \\ \hline \end{array} \quad \begin{array}{r} 6 \\ 6 \\ +\ \square \\ \hline \end{array} \quad \begin{array}{r} 7 \\ 3 \\ +\ \square \\ \hline \end{array}$$

Reasoning

Ring the one in each pair that you think has
the greater sum. Then solve to check.

4.
$$\begin{array}{r} 7 \\ 3 \\ +\ 6 \\ \hline \end{array} \qquad \begin{array}{r} 8 \\ 2 \\ +\ 5 \\ \hline \end{array}$$

5.
$$\begin{array}{r} 4 \\ 4 \\ +\ 2 \\ \hline \end{array} \qquad \begin{array}{r} 3 \\ 4 \\ +\ 4 \\ \hline \end{array}$$

Problem-Solving Strategy

Make a Table

Some children voted for their favorite birds. Then they made this table.

Our Favorite Birds			
	Grade 1	**Grade 2**	**Grade 3**
duck	10	7	3
owl	12	13	7
eagle	9	8	15

Read the table. Answer these questions about it.

1. How many children in Grade 1 like ducks best?   __10__ children

2. How many children in Grade 2 like owls best?   ____ children

3. How many children in Grade 3 like eagles best?   ____ children

4. How many children in all like ducks best?   ____ children

Story Corner

5. Write a question about the table. Give it to a friend to answer.

_____

- - - - - - - - - - - - - - - - - - - -
_____

- - - - - - - - - - - - - - - - - - - -
_____

Sums and Differences to 14

Write the addition facts that help.
Then complete the subtraction facts.

1.
```
  12        7
 - 5      + 5
 ───      ───
   7       12
```
```
  14
 - 5
 ───
```
```
  10
 - 6
 ───
```

2.
```
   9
 - 3
 ───
```
```
  13
 - 8
 ───
```
```
  11
 - 4
 ───
```

3.
```
  12
 - 8
 ───
```
```
  14
 - 7
 ───
```
```
  13
 - 6
 ───
```

4.
```
  11
 - 9
 ───
```
```
   8
 - 6
 ───
```
```
  14
 - 8
 ───
```

Problem Solving

5. Jon filled 4 bags with leaves. His mother filled 5 bags. How many bags in all did they fill?

_____ bags

6. Mollie washed 12 glasses. Her brother washed 6 glasses. How many more glasses did Mollie wash?

_____ more glasses

Sums and Differences to 18

Write the sum and difference for each pair.

1.

$\begin{array}{r} 4 \\ + 8 \\ \hline 12 \end{array}$ $\begin{array}{r} 12 \\ - 8 \\ \hline 4 \end{array}$ $\begin{array}{r} 8 \\ + 8 \\ \hline \end{array}$ $\begin{array}{r} 16 \\ - 8 \\ \hline \end{array}$ $\begin{array}{r} 8 \\ + 5 \\ \hline \end{array}$ $\begin{array}{r} 13 \\ - 5 \\ \hline \end{array}$

2.

$\begin{array}{r} 9 \\ + 8 \\ \hline \end{array}$ $\begin{array}{r} 17 \\ - 8 \\ \hline \end{array}$ $\begin{array}{r} 7 \\ + 8 \\ \hline \end{array}$ $\begin{array}{r} 15 \\ - 8 \\ \hline \end{array}$ $\begin{array}{r} 2 \\ + 9 \\ \hline \end{array}$ $\begin{array}{r} 11 \\ - 9 \\ \hline \end{array}$

3.

$\begin{array}{r} 7 \\ + 7 \\ \hline \end{array}$ $\begin{array}{r} 14 \\ - 7 \\ \hline \end{array}$ $\begin{array}{r} 6 \\ + 9 \\ \hline \end{array}$ $\begin{array}{r} 15 \\ - 9 \\ \hline \end{array}$ $\begin{array}{r} 9 \\ + 9 \\ \hline \end{array}$ $\begin{array}{r} 18 \\ - 9 \\ \hline \end{array}$

Reasoning

Which way would you use to find
each sum? Draw a line to match.

4. $9 + 7 = ?$ •

5. $9 + 2 = ?$ •

6. $6 + 6 = ?$ •

• Add doubles.

• Count on.

• Make a 10.

Fact Families

Write each fact family.

1.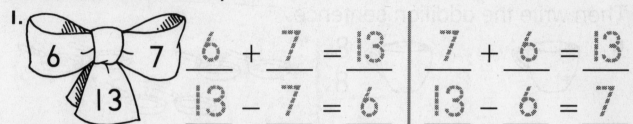

$6 + 7 = 13$ | $7 + 6 = 13$
$13 - 7 = 6$ | $13 - 6 = 7$

2.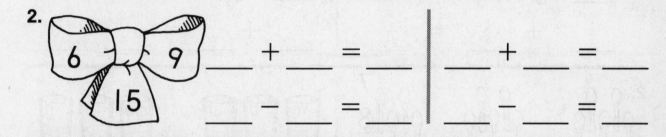

____ + ____ = ____ | ____ + ____ = ____
____ − ____ = ____ | ____ − ____ = ____

3.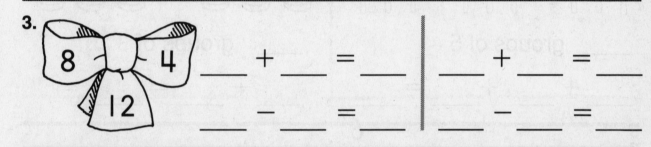

____ + ____ = ____ | ____ + ____ = ____
____ − ____ = ____ | ____ − ____ = ____

4.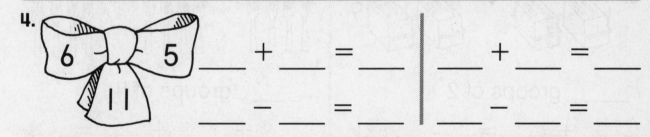

____ + ____ = ____ | ____ + ____ = ____
____ − ____ = ____ | ____ − ____ = ____

Number Sense

5. Ring an estimate. Then use a to solve.

There are 9 children swimming.
8 more come.
Then 10 of them leave.
How many children are swimming?

more than 9

fewer than 9

_____ children

Making Equal Groups

Write how many groups.
Then write the addition sentence.

1.

__2__ groups of 1   ____ groups of 2

__1__ + __1__ = __2__   ___ + ___ + ___ = ___

2.

____ groups of 5   ____ groups of 3

___ + ___ + ___ = ___   ___ + ___ = ___

3.

____ groups of 2   ____ groups of 4

___ + ___ = ___   ___ + ___ + ___ = ___

Reasoning

4. Ring the child who has more stones.

I collected 4 stones every day for 2 days.

I collected 2 stones every day for 5 days.

Problem-Solving Strategy

Make a Model

Work with a group.
Use counters to model each problem.
Give an equal number to each child in the group.
Write how many counters each child gets.

1. There are 8 toy cars.
There are 4 children.
How many toy cars does
each child get? Each

   child gets __2__ cars.

2. There are 6 blocks.
There are 2 children.
How many blocks does
each child get? Each

   child gets _____ blocks.

3. There are 12 books.
There are 3 children.
How many books does
each child get? Each

   child gets _____ books.

4. There are 15 crayons.
There are 5 children.
How many crayons does
each child get? Each

   child gets _____ crayons

Reasoning

5. Ring the child who has fewer shells.

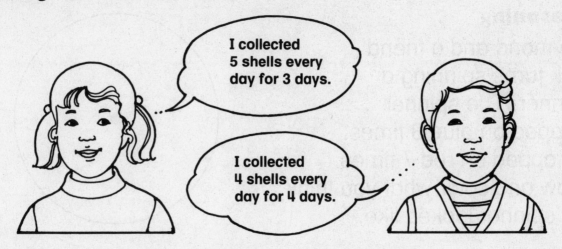

I collected
5 shells every
day for 3 days.

I collected
4 shells every
day for 4 days.

Tallying Events

Work with a friend.
Use a pencil and a paper clip
to make a spinner. Predict
which color the spinner
will stop on most often.
Ring the color.

gray   black   white

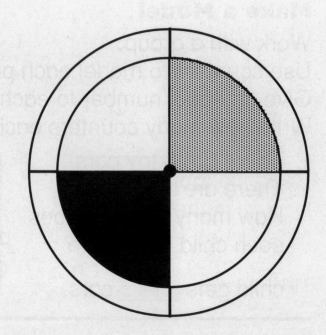

Try it. Take turns
spinning the paper clip.
Spin 10 times.
Make a tally mark
after each spin.

	Tally Marks	Total
gray		
black		
white		

Reasoning

Raymond and a friend
took turns spinning a
spinner. The spinner
stopped on blue 3 times.
It stopped on red 7 times.
Draw and color what you think
the spinner looked like.

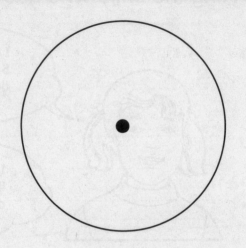

Graphing Data

○	||||
△	|||| |||
□	|||

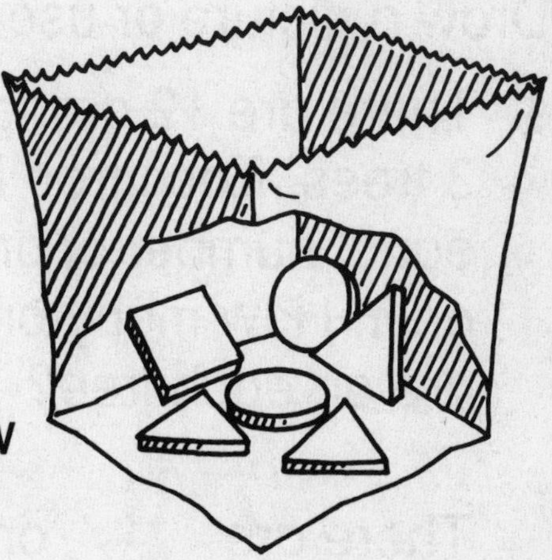

Read the table.
Now fill in the graph below to show how many times each shape was picked.

Color Graph

○											
△											
□											

0   1   2   3   4   5   6   7   8   9   10

2. Which shape was picked most often? _____

3. How many picks were made in all? _____ picks

Story Corner

4. Write a question about the graph.
   Give it to a friend to answer.

_____

_____

_____

_____

Problem Solving

Choose the Strategy

Draw a picture or use counters to solve.

1. There are 12 oranges. There are
3 trees. Each tree has an
equal number of oranges
on it. How many oranges
are on each tree?

   There are ___4___ oranges on each tree.

2. There are 5 ears of corn in
the brown bag.
There are 7 ears of corn in
the white bag.
How many ears of corn are
in both bags?

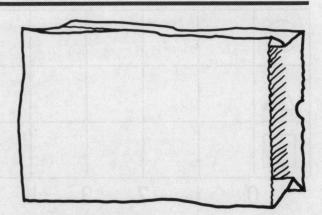

   There are _____ ears of corn in both bags.

3. Lindy had 17 grapes. She ate
8 of them. How many
grapes does Lindy
have left?

   Lindy has _____ grapes left.

Number Sense

4. Ring the better estimate. There are
2 groups of 4 birds. One group
flies away. How many birds are left?

   more than 8

   fewer than 8

Core Skills: Math, Grade 1, Answer Key

Page 1
1. Cowboy hat
2. Polka dot hat
3. Baseball cap
4. Striped hat
5. Ring middle group.

Page 2
1. Ring first hat.
2. Ring second balloon.
3. Ring first kite.
4. Ring second box.
5. ABBABB

Page 3
1–4. Answers will vary.
5. Ring first group.

Page 4
Ring birds, rabbits, squirrels, and turtles.
1. 2
2. 1
3. 3
4. Ring first picture.

Page 5
1. 5, 4, 5
2. 4, 3, 5
3. 2, 4, 3
4. Ring middle group.
   Draw an X on the first and last groups.

Page 6
1. 3
2. 4
3. 2
4. 5
5. 4
6. 3
7. Ring second purse; draw an X on the first purse.

Page 7
1. 3
2. 0
3. 2
4. 0
5. 1
6. 4
7. Ring middle group.
   Draw an X on the first and last groups.

Page 8
1. triangle, circle, triangle
2. circle, triangle, triangle
3. triangle, circle, circle
4. triangle, circle, triangle
5. circle, triangle, circle
6. triangle, triangle, circle
7. triangle, triangle, circle
8. No

Page 9
1. 6, six
2. 4, four
3. 0, zero
4. 5, five
5. 7, seven
6. 3, three
7. Ring second and last groups; draw an X on the first and third groups.

Page 10
1–3. Check work.

Page 11
1. nine, 9
2. seven, 7
3. ten, 10
4. eight, 8
5. Ring middle group.

Page 12
1. 5
2. 6
3. 10
4. 7
5. 2
6. 4
7. 8, 7, 6, 3, 1
8. 9, 8, 5, 4, 3, 2
9. Ring last group.

Page 13
1. Ring 6; 5
2. 4; ring 9
3. 5; ring 3
4. Ring 7; 9
5. six
6. ten

Page 14
1. Check drawings.
2. Ring square.
3. Ring rectangle.

Page 15
1. 4, 1; 5
2. 2, 1; 3
3. 5, 1; 6
4. 4
5. 5

Page 16
1. $2 + 1 = 3$
2. $2 + 2 = 4$
3. $4 + 1 = 5$
4. $3 + 2 = 5$
5. $5 + 1 = 6$
6. $1 + 2 = 3$
7. $2 + 2 = 4$

Page 17
1–3. Check drawings.
4. Ring first and middle drawings.

Page 18
1–6. Check work.
1. 2
2. 3
3. 5
4. 1
5. 6
6. 4
7. less than 5

Page 19
1–3. Check drawings.
1. 3
2. 5
3. 6
4. Check drawing.

Page 20
1. $1 + 2$
2. $2 + 1$
3. $0 + 3$
4. $3 + 0$
5. $1 + 3$
6. $3 + 1$
7. $0 + 4$
8. $4 + 0$
9. $2 + 2$
10. 7, 5; ring 5.

Core Skills: Math, Grade 1, Answer Key (cont.)

Page 21
1. 2 + 3
2. 3 + 2
3. 1 + 4
4. 4 + 1
5. 0 + 5
6. 5 + 0
7. 2 + 4
8. 4 + 2
9. 1 + 5
10. 5 + 1
11. 0 + 6
12. 6 + 0
13. 3 + 3
14. No

Page 22
1. 1 + 3 = 4
2. 2 + 4 = 6
3. 3 + 2 = 5
4. less than 5¢

Page 23
1. 3 + 2 = 5
2. 4 + 1 = 5
3. 5 + 0 = 5
4. 2 + 2 = 4
5. Ring first and second groups.

Page 24
1. 3, 1; 2
2. 5, 1; 4
3. 2, 1; 1
4. 3, 1, 2

Page 25
1. 4 − 2 = 2
2. 5 − 2 = 3
3. 6 − 2 = 4
4. 3 − 1 = 2
5. 5 − 1 = 4
6. 2 − 1 = 1
7. 5, 3, 2
8. 6, 4, 2

Page 26
1. 2
2. 0
3. 0
4. 4
5. 5
6. 6
7. 0
8. 0
9. 2

Page 27
1. 2
2. 5
3. 3
4. 3
5. 4
6. 5
7. 6 − 3 = 3

Page 28
1. Subtract
2. Add
3. 4 − 1 = 3
4. 2 + 3 = 5
5. 6 − 0 = 6
6. 4 + 1 = 5
7. +, −, +

Page 29
1–5. Order of responses will vary.
1. 2, 2
2. 4, 0
3. 0, 4
4. 1, 3
5. 3, 1
6. 2, 5, 0
7. 0, 1, 1
8. 1, 1, 2
9. 0, 3, 5
10. 3, 3, 0
11. less than 9

Page 30
1–6. Order of responses will vary.
1. 5, 0
2. 0, 5
3. 3, 2
4. 4, 1
5. 1, 4
6. 2, 3
7. 3, 4, 5
8. 3, 4, 5
9. 4, 3, 2
10. 4, 3, 2
11. Rings may vary. 7, 8, 9

Page 31
1. 2
2. 4
3. 6
4. 1
5. 0
6. 5
7. 2
8. 1
9. Check drawings.

Page 32
1. 6, 5, 1
2. 6, 2, 4
3. 5, 2, 3
4. more than 4, less than 4, more than 3, less than 3

Page 33
1. How many are left?
2. How many in all?
3. How many in all?
4. How many are left?
5. How many are left?
6. How many in all?
7. 4 − 1 = 3

Page 34
1. 5, 6
2. 9, 7
3. 6, 4
4. 7, 8, 9
5. 10, 9, 8
6. 10 + 2

Page 35
1. 5, 7, 3, 10
2. 3, 6, 9, 2, 10, 8
3. 6, 10, 8, 4, 7, 9
4. 9, 8, 10, 10, 9, 8
5. 7, 6, 9, 10, 7, 6
6. 9 + 1

Page 36
1. 7
2. 9
3. 9
4. 8
5. 7
6. 9
7. 10

Page 37
1. 6 + 3 = 9, 4 + 2 = 6, 5 + 3 = 8
2. 8 + 2 = 10, 5 + 2 = 7, 3 + 3 = 6
3. Answers will vary.

Core Skills: Math, Grade 1, Answer Key (cont.)

Page 38
1. Ring 9, 10; ring 6, 8;
   ring 3, 5; ring 4, 6;
   ring 4, 7; ring 7, 9
2. Ring 4, 5; ring 8, 10;
   ring 5, 8; ring 4, 5;
   ring 5, 6; ring 7, 10
3. 1 + 8, 9; 10
4. 8; 2 + 5 = 7
5. 7; 4 + 2 = 6

Page 39
1. 4, 8; 1, 2
2. 0, 0; 5, 10
3. 6, 2, 8, 4, 0, 10
4. 8; 8; ring 3 + 3, 6;
   ring 0 + 0, 0; 9; ring 5 + 5, 10
5. ring 4 + 4, 8; 10; 8;
   ring 2 + 2, 4; 7; ring 1 + 1, 2
6. 7

Page 40
Check table.
Peter and Jane

Page 41
1. 6 + 4 = 10; 3 + 7 = 10
2. 7 + 1 = 8; 2 + 6 = 8
3. 10, 8, 8, 10, 9, 7
4. 9, 10, 9, 10, 9, 10
5. Ring 1 and 4; 5 + 5 = 10.

Page 42
1–6. Check coloring.
7. Ring second and last
   pictures.

Page 43
1. Draw a line through "There
   are 2 trucks on the road,"
   4 + 3 = 7; 7.
2. Draw a line through "He
   sees a train, too,"
   4 + 4 = 8; 8.
3. Draw a line through "Anna
   counts 5 trees,"
   3 + 6 = 9; 9.
4. Answers will vary.

Page 44
1. 3, 2, 4
2. 5, 3, 7
3. 4, 5, 2
4. 7, 1, 9
5. 6, 8, 8
6. 4
7. 6

Page 45
1. 7, 9, 3, 4, 2, 5
2. 1, 8, 3, 2, 7, 6
3. 6, 7, 8, 4, 4, 5
4. 2

Page 46
1. Check coloring; 2, 7, 6; 5, 7,
   6; 4, 3, 5
2. 6, 2, 2, 4, 8, 4
3. 6; ring 7 – 3, 4
4. 7; ring 8 – 2, 6
5. 7; ring 9 – 3, 6

Page 47
1. 5
2. 3
3. 5
4. 6
5. 3
6. 6
7. Stories will vary.

Page 48
1. 5, 1, 3, 0, 5, 3
2. 7, 2, 3, 1, 7, 3
3. 8, 2, 5, 2, 6, 3
4. 4, 3, 2, 3, 9, 1
5. Ring child on far left.

Page 49
1. 5 + 1 = 6; 6 – 1 = 5
2. 7 + 2 = 9; 9 – 2 = 7
3. 6 + 3 = 9; 9 – 3 = 6
4. 4 + 4 = 8; 8 – 4 = 4
5. Add

Page 50
1. 6, 6, 5, 1; 5, 1, 6; 4, 4, 3, 1;
   3, 1, 4; 5, 5, 2, 3; 2, 3, 5
2. 8, 8, 6, ring 7 – 2, 5, 2
3. 8, 8, ring 4 + 3, 7, 3, 5
4. 3, 2

Page 51
1–6. Ring 1, 3, 4, 6
7. 2

Page 52
1. 5, 4
2. 3, 3
3. 4, 3
4. 5, 3
5. Ring middle pair of cubes.

Page 53
1–5. Check coloring.
6. cube

Page 54
1. Ring first four shapes.
2. Draw an X on the first,
   middle, and last shapes.
3. Color first four shapes.
4. Ring cone; No shapes can
   be stacked on the point of
   the cone.

Page 55
1. rectangle, rectangular cube;
   triangle, pyramid; circle,
   cylinder; square, cube
2. 8

Page 56
1–3. Check work.
4. diamond

Page 57
1–3. Check work.
4. C, G, N, S

Page 58
1–6. Check coloring.
1. 3, 3
2. 4, 4
3. 8, 8
4. 5, 5
5. 3, 3
6. 4, 4
7. open figure

Page 59
1. cube—8; cone—3;
   cylinder—5;
   rectangular prism—6
2. W

Page 60
1–8. Check work.
9. Ring middle drawing.

Page 61
1. Ring first, second, and third
   drawings.
2. Ring first, fourth, and fifth
   drawings.
3. Ring first, third, and fifth
   drawings.
4. Ring first, second, and third
   drawings.
5. Ring smaller, same, and
   bigger. (respectively)

Core Skills: Math, Grade 1, Answer Key (cont.)

Page 62
1. middle pattern
2. top pattern
3. bottom pattern
4. Underline bottom row.

Page 63
1. red
2. blue
3. red
4. 1

Page 64
1. blue
2. blue
3. green
4. 2

Page 65
1. Ring all groups. 3, 30
2. Ring all groups. 2, 20
3. Ring all groups. 5, 50
4. 4 groups of 10

Page 66
1. 1, 1; 11
2. 1, 2; 12
3. 1, 6; 16
4. 2, 0; 20
5. fewer than 10

Page 67
1. 30
2. 50
3. 7
4. 40
5. 21

Page 68
1. 65, 36, 54
2. 36
3. 80
4. 54
5. 79
6. Ring first group.

Page 69
1. 74, 84, 94
2. 65
3. 29
4. 41
5. 98
6. 7 tens 6 ones

Page 70
1–3. Check work.
1. 70
2. 50
3. 40
4. 60

Page 71
1. 12
2. 35
3. 63
4. 44
5. Ring first group.

Page 72
1–2. Check work.
1. 1, 5
2. 2, 4
3. Ring first group.

Page 73
1–4. Ring in blue.
1. 55
2. 48
3. 82
4. 69
5. Ring in red: 34, 12, 41, 29, 21, 22, 44, 20, 38.

Page 74
1. 21, 23; 46, 48; 96, 98
2. 38, 13, 21; 92, 26, 79; 23, 87, 33; 62, 45, 81
3. Yes
4. Yes

Page 75
1. 14, 17, 19
2. 21, 24, 26, 27, 29
3. 38, 40, 41, 42, 44, 46
4. 92, 93, 97, 98, 99
5. 51, 53, 55, 56, 57, 60
6. 84, 85

Page 76
1. 62, 63, 64, 66, 68, 69, 70
2. 58, 59, 60, 62, 63, 64, 65
3. 21, 22, 25, 26, 27, 28, 29
4. 47, 48, 49, 51, 52, 53
5. 33, 35, 36, 37, 40, 41
6. 90, 91, 93, 94, 96, 98
7. 15, 16, 17, 18, 19

Page 77
1. 5, 10, 15, 20, 25
2. 10, 20, 30, 40, 50
3. 61

Page 78
1–2. Check work.
3. can't tell

Page 79
1. 4, 2
2. 25, 30, 35
3. 50
4. 7

Page 80
1. $3 + 4 = 7, 7 - 4 = 3$
2. $6 + 2 = 8, 8 - 2 = 6$
3. $4 + 6 = 10, 10 - 6 = 4$
4. $5 + 5 = 10, 10 - 5 = 5$
5. $6 + 3 = 9, 9 - 3 = 6$
6. $7 - 2 = 5$

Page 81
1. Ring 6, 8; ring 6, 9; ring 7, 10; ring 8, 9; ring 7, 9; ring 9, 12.
2. Ring 9, 10; ring 9, 11; ring 8, 10; ring 5, 8; ring 8, 11; ring 5, 7.
3. Ring 6, 7; ring 7, 10; ring 7, 8; ring 9, 11; ring 9, 12; ring 6, 9.
4. 7

Page 82
1. Ring $3 + 3$, 6; 8; 11
2. 6; ring $6 + 6$, 12; ring $4 + 4$, 8
3. Ring $2 + 2$, 4; ring $5 + 5$, 10; 8
4. Ring $1 + 1$, 2; 8; 10; 10; ring $3 + 3$, 6; 9
5. 8; ring $5 + 5$, 10; ring $4 + 4$, 8; 9; 11; ring $6 + 6$, 12
6. 4, 4, 8; 8

Page 83
1. 10, 11, 5, 2, 8, 3
2. 9, 6, 0, 7, 4, 1
3. 9
4. 1
5. 5
6. 3
7. 11
8. 7

Page 84
1. 10, 10, 10, 11, 9, 9
2. 6, 12, 8, 12, 11, 11
3. less than 10; more than 10

Page 85
1–4. Answers will vary.

Page 86
1. 9, 7, 6, 6, 5, 8
2. 9, 8, 9, 7, 4, 6
3. 8, 7, 5, 5, 9, 4
4. Ring 50 − 1.

Page 87
1. 1, 3, 2, 3
2. 2, 2, 1, 3
3. 1, 2, 1, 3, 2, 2
4. 4, 3, 1, 2, 3, 2
5. Check work: 3, 9, 3, 8, 7, 2

Page 88
1. 11, 6
2. 11, 7
3. 10, 5
4. 12, 8
5. 11, 9
6. 12, 6
7. 10, 7
8. 12, 7
9. Add

Page 89
1. 10, 10, ring 6 + 3 = 9, 3, 7
2. 9, 9, 1, ring 8 − 1 = 7, 8
3. Ring 2 + 6 = 8, 9, 9, 2, 7
4. 8, 8, 3, ring 9 − 5 = 4, 5
5. 5

Page 90
1. 5 + 6 = 11; 4 + 7 = 11; 5 + 7 = 12
2. 7, 5; 8, 4; 6, 6
3. Nan, Ricky

Page 91
1–5. Answers will vary.

Page 92
1. Add, 9 + 3 = 12, 12
2. Subtract, 9 − 5 = 4, 4
3. Subtract, 11 − 3 = 8, 8
4. Check work.

Page 93
1–4. Answers will vary.
5. Cross out pen.

Page 94
1–4. Answers will vary.
5. Ring second answer.

Page 95
1. 5
2. 2
3. 4
4. 1
5. rectangle
6. 2 sides are 1 inch tall. 2 sides are 2 inches long.

Page 96
1–6. Answers will vary.

Page 97
1–4. Answers will vary.
5. 20

Page 98
1. Ring notebook.
2. Ring book.
3. Ring paste.
4. Ring crayons.
5. pan

Page 99
1–4. Answers will vary.
5. Ring second picture.

Page 100
1. Ring teapot.
2. Ring hamburger.
3. Ring sink.
4. Ring pot.
5. Ring second thermometer.

Page 101
1. Answers will vary.
2. Questions will vary.

Page 102
1. Ring second banana.
2. Ring first watermelon.
3. Ring first plate.
4. Ring second plate.
5. Ring top bag.
6. Ring top loaf.
7. Check drawing.

Page 103
1–4. Check drawings.
5. Check coloring.
6. 2

Page 104
1. $\frac{1}{3}$, $\frac{1}{2}$, $\frac{1}{3}$
2. $\frac{1}{2}$, $\frac{1}{3}$, $\frac{1}{3}$
3–4. Check coloring.
5. $\frac{1}{2}$

Page 105
1. $\frac{1}{3}$, $\frac{1}{4}$, $\frac{1}{2}$
2. $\frac{1}{4}$, $\frac{1}{2}$, $\frac{1}{3}$
3. Check coloring.
4. $\frac{1}{3}$

Page 106
1–6. Check coloring.
7. $\frac{1}{3}$

Page 107
1. bottom graph
2. top graph
3. middle graph
4–5. Check drawings.
6. $\frac{2}{3}$

Page 108
1. Ring second glass in green; ring fourth glass in red.
2. Ring first pencil in green; ring third pencil in red.
3. Ring second paper in red; ring third paper in green.
4. Stories will vary.

Page 109
1. Ring second picture.
2. Ring second picture.
3. Ring first picture.
4. Ring second picture.
5. Ring middle picture.

Page 110
1. 3
2. 7
3. 10
4. 8
5. 5
6. 9
7. 6

Page 111
1. Check answers.
2. 6:00, 4:00, 2:00
3. 12:00

Page 112
1–3. Answers will vary.
4. more than 1 hour

Page 113
1. 8:00, 12:30, 1:30
2. 2:30, 9:00, 5:00
3. Check answers.
4. more than 30 minutes

Core Skills: Math, Grade 1, Answer Key (cont.)

Page 114
Check calendar.
1–4. Answers depend on month.
5. Answer depends on months compared.

Page 115
1–3. Check answers.
4. Stories will vary.

Page 116
1–4. Check work.
5. Ring second picture.
6. Ring first picture.

Page 117
1–6. Check work.
7. 4 dimes

Page 118
1. 20
2. 8
3. 40
4. 25, ring quarter
5. 25, ring nickels
6. 70
7. 25¢

Page 119
1. 10, 20, 30, 31, 32; 32
2. 5, 10, 11, 12, 13; 13
3. 55
4. 27
5. 2 dimes 9 pennies

Page 120
1. 25, 30, 35, 36, 37; 37
2. 25, 35, 45, 50; 50
3. 25, 35, 40, 45, 46; 46
4. 25, 35, 45, 50, 55, 56; 56
5. Ring 2 dimes, 1 nickel, and 1 quarter.

Page 121
1–2. Answers will vary.
3–4. Check work.
5. Yes

Page 122
1. 50
2. 30
3. 45
4. 42
5. Answers may vary. Possible answer: Give: 4 dimes, 2 nickels; Take: 2 quarters.

Page 123
1. 9, 10, 11, 12
2. 5, 6, 7, 8
3. bottom, top, middle
4. middle, bottom, top
5. 4
6. 5

Page 124
1–4. Check work.
1. 14
2. 26
3. 33
4. 18
5. more than 30
6. between 10 and 30

Page 125
1. 40 + 20 = 60
2. 30 + 30 = 60
3. 30 + 10 = 40
4. 60 + 20 = 80
5. 40 + 40 = 80
6. 10 + 50 = 60
7. bottom, top, middle
8. bottom, top, middle

Page 126
1–10. Answers will vary.
11. 37
12. 47

Page 127
1. 6, 9; 4, 8; 4, 5; 8, 7
2. 79, 36, 95, 87, 97
3. 80; more than 80; less than 80
4. 20; less than 20; more than 20

Page 128
1. 80, 70, 50, 40, 70
2. 60, 20, 90, 20, 90
3. 90, 90, 30, 30, 70
4. 53, 63, 73, 83, 93
5. 33, 43, 53, 63, 73

Page 129
1–10. Answers will vary.
11. 52
12. 65

Page 130
1. 2, 1; 3, 3; 3; 1, 4
2. 2, 2; 4, 7; 2, 2; 1, 3
3. 40, 21, 63, 14, 32
4. 40; less than 40; more than 40

Page 131
Check work.
1. 65 + 23
2. 67 – 5

Page 132
1. 4 spaceships
2. 32 pennies
3. 8 years old
4. 38 children
5. 30 trips

Page 133
1. about 80¢; 85
2. about 20¢; 23
3. about 30¢; 34
4. Answers will vary.

Page 134
1. 4, 3
2. 7, 4
3. 7

Page 135
1. 2, 1; 4, 2; 6, 3
2. 8, 4; 10, 5; 12, 6
3. 14, 7; 16, 8; 18, 9

Page 136
1. 3
2. 9
3. 1
4. 16, 17
5. 14, 15
6. 10, 6, 13, 9, 4, 7
7. 5, 16, 11, 17, 8, 12
8. 11
9. 13

Page 137
1. 7
2. 13
3. 15
4. 17
5. 11
6. 18, 13, 7, 2, 17, 14
7. 16, 1, 9, 15, 8, 10
8. Check work.

Page 138
1. 11, 14, 12, 12, 14, 13
2. 15, 11, 12, 11, 13, 16
3. 14, 13, 16, 11, 11, 12
4. 1
5. 2

Core Skills: Math, Grade 1, Answer Key (cont.)

Page 139
1–3. Answers will vary.
4. 16, 15
5. 10, 11

Page 140
1. 10
2. 13
3. 15
4. 20
5. Questions will vary.

Page 141
1–4. Order of addends may vary.
1. 7, 7 + 5 = 12; 9, 9 + 5 = 14; 4, 4 + 6 = 10
2. 6, 6 + 3 = 9; 5, 5 + 8 = 13; 7, 7 + 4 = 11
3. 4, 4 + 8 = 12; 7, 7 + 7 = 14; 7, 7 + 6 = 13
4. 2, 2 + 9 = 11; 2, 2 + 6 = 8; 6, 6 + 8 = 14
5. 9
6. 6

Page 142
1. 12, 4; 16, 8; 13, 8
2. 17, 9; 15, 7; 11, 2
3. 14, 7; 15, 6; 18, 9
4. Answers may vary.

Page 143
1. 6 + 7 = 13, 13 − 7 = 6, 7 + 6 = 13, 13 − 6 = 7
2. 6 + 9 = 15, 15 − 9 = 6, 9 + 6 = 15, 15 − 6 = 9
3. 8 + 4 = 12, 12 − 4 = 8, 4 + 8 = 12, 12 − 8 = 4
4. 6 + 5 = 11, 11 − 5 = 6, 5 + 6 = 11, 11 − 6 = 5
5. fewer than 9; 7

Page 144
1. 2, 1 + 1 = 2; 3, 2 + 2 + 2 = 6
2. 3, 5 + 5 + 5 = 15; 2, 3 + 3 = 6
3. 2, 2 + 2 = 4; 3, 4 + 4 + 4 = 12
4. Ring second child.

Page 145
1. 2
2. 3
3. 4
4. 3
5. Ring first child.

Page 146
White
Predictions and answers will vary.
Spinners will vary, but the longer part should be red.

Page 147
1. Check graphs.
2. triangle
3. 16
4. Questions will vary.

Page 148
1. 4
2. 12
3. 9
4. fewer than 8